PEACE OF MIND

PEACE OF MIND

A book of calm for
busy mums

GEORGINA RODGERS

HODDER &
STOUGHTON

First published in Great Britain in 2016 by
Hodder & Stoughton

An Hachette UK company

2

Copyright © Georgina Rodgers 2016
Illustrations pages 74, 92, 116, 135, 158, 178, 208, 227, 241 by Saffron Stocker

A CIP catalogue record for this title is available from the British Library

Hardback ISBN 978 1 473 63551 7
eBook ISBN 978 1 473 63552 4

Typeset in Avenir by Hewer Text UK Ltd, Edinburgh

Printed and bound by CPI Group (UK) Ltd, Croydon, CR0 4YY

Hodder & Stoughton policy is to use papers that are natural, renewable
and recyclable products and made from wood grown in sustainable forests.
The logging and manufacturing processes are expected to conform to the
environmental regulations of the country of origin.

Hodder & Stoughton Ltd
Carmelite House
50 Victoria Embankment
London EC4Y 0DZ

www.hodder.co.uk

*To my own marvellous mum and
my girls, Arabella and Alice,
who make my world shine brighter*

CONTENTS

INTRODUCTION

Mother (ˈmʌðə)

noun

oving partner, outstanding teacher, personal chef, kind nurse, dependable cleaner, chief negotiator, on-call taxi driver, loyal friend, diligent laundry maid, trusted housekeeper, head cheerleader, motivational speaker, expert event planner . . . mothers everywhere do thousands of small things every day for their loved ones and barely have time to pause; to take time out for themselves, just breathe and find inner calm.

As a mum of two young children, I sometimes feel like I just never, ever stop. My fatigued brain seems to whir constantly with an all-encompassing jumble of thoughts ranging from whether fish fingers for the third time in a week is bad for my three-year-old, to whether I can really make that important work phone call while my six-month-old bobs about madly in her baby bouncer next to my desk.

The seeds of an idea for this book were sown in the early sleep-deprived days after my second daughter was born, when I was having a rough time. I felt like I was dangling precariously off the back of some sort of feeding, nappy-changing, cuddling, washing, working treadmill, set on sprint mode. I was endlessly trying to cram more and more into less time, obsessed with doing everything at breakneck speed. I found myself falling into bed at night, completely drained, but instead of dropping off, I would lie awake for hours with my brain like a spinning top.

Like most mothers, I have wildly unrealistic expectations of myself and am hard on myself when I do not live up to my ideals. As women and mothers, we seem to have a lot of time to care for, nurture and encourage our children, family, friends and others around us, yet all too often we're not so kind to ourselves. Like most people, I had heard about mindfulness and I wondered how it could help me and other mums like me.

It's been an interesting journey reading and learning about mindfulness and other ways to feel calmer and more centred. There are many differing schools of thought about areas of mindfulness and meditation, with new research being released all the time. There are many ways to practise mindfulness and being calm. Whether you take some ideas from this book, find yourself downloading one of the many apps available online or take a local meditation class, it is all positive. I have learned that not only is being calm good for your personal health, but it can enrich your life in many ways and make you a happier and more settled mother.

I'm certainly no mindfulness guru, just a normal, busy working mum, but these days I'm trying to practise what I preach. From noticing the patterns of the clouds in the sky when I push the swings at the park, to really tasting chocolate when I eat it, mindfulness has made me more aware of my own emotions and feelings. It's not easy and I often find my mind wandering back to thoughts of deadlines, dinners and dramas, but I am determined to stick with it.

If you are a strung-out and busy mother, then this book is for you. Whether you have two minutes or twenty minutes, this journal will help to guide you towards a calmer life. It doesn't need to be read in a linear way – you can dip in and out of it as you please. As well as mindfulness exercises and meditations, there are inspirational quotes, poems and fascinating research to ponder on, and colouring in, craft ideas and gratitude lists, so you can nurture your creative side.

It is a non-prescriptive, practical and motivational guide to help you find your way to achieving inner calm, balance and contentment in all areas of your life, from your relationships, through to your work, travels and home life. I hope this journal will also act as a keepsake, where some of your most treasured and important memories will be kept for ever.

I also aim to inspire you to find your own artistic streak and focus on appreciating life, slowing down and observing the world around you with fresh eyes . . . To belly-laugh with your child, switch off the Wi-Fi, pick a strawberry and savour it in your mouth, paddle in the sea, fly a kite, read beautiful poems, smile often . . .

CHAPTER 1

MINDFULNESS

'Sometimes you will
never know the value
of something until
it is a memory.'

DR SEUSS

GOING FROM MIND FULL
TO MINDFUL . . .

Before writing this book, I had never meditated. I just can't sit still for long enough. I was rubbish at yoga: inflexible, and the second I tried to hold a pose, my mind wandered: planning, thinking, analysing past events or agonising over future decisions. Mindfulness works for busy people because it is a way of living; it is not a goal, a place to get to, or another thing on the 'to-do' list. Mindfulness allows for imperfections and, while it is often equated with meditation, it is a much broader concept. It is simply a different way of viewing the world.

At its core, mindfulness encourages us to 'be present' in our own lives when we are distracted by intrusive thoughts of past events, or worries about the future. Reining in thoughts is harder than it sounds; in my mind it's like trying to round up a dozen wayward toddlers in a busy playground. According to scientists, we have between 60,000 and 80,000 thoughts a day and most are repetitive – ones that we had the day before and will continue to have. One study showed that our minds are wandering for nearly as much time as they are actually focused on what is in front of us. Worse than that, we seem to be less happy in those moments when our minds are drifting.

Mindfulness is a way of seeing what is happening at that moment in time. It doesn't change what is happening in our lives or at that point, but it can help us respond to the events that take place in a calmer way, benefitting our minds, our health and our relationships.

The practice is about focusing on each moment – you observe your thoughts as they come into your mind, but let go of holding on to them or struggling against them. Our brains produce thoughts – that is a fact of life. You don't try to stop your thoughts; you simply allow the thoughts to come and go, like bubbles popping in the air or a string of pearls running through your mind. Your attention can only be on one thing at a time, so if you are totally focused on the here and now, such as what you can see, smell and hear, then your attention isn't feeding your anxieties and worries and you begin to break this chain. If you do not give them any attention, they slowly start to calm and eventually cease to exist entirely. With time, experts say, being mindful becomes easier and you will get less and less lost in negative and unnecessary thought patterns. The more aware you become of what you tend to focus on, the more you learn about yourself.

Being mindful means that you do not judge your thoughts and do not decide that they are either 'right' or 'wrong'. This allows you to bring your attention fully to that moment and not cling on to negative feelings. You can catch critical thought patterns before they tip you into a downward spiral.

Living in the moment allows you to really appreciate the world around you. So when you are walking in the park, you might notice the distinct colour of the leaves on the trees; the birds flying overhead or singing in the trees; the feel of the earth beneath your soles; the shrieks of nearby children – rather than your attention being hijacked by thoughts about the stack of laundry at home, when you might do an online supermarket shop, office politics at your work or any other deeper worries.

Learning to be mindful takes time and persistence but is not complicated and is not something you can either make a success of or fail at. It is worth remembering that even when it feels really hard, you will have have benefitted psychologically and learned something about yourself. According to experts, our minds will grow whatever seeds we plant in them, so, just as working out at the gym makes us fitter and trains our muscles to lift heavy weights, mindfulness trains the brain to lift our worries off our shoulders, giving us greater clarity and putting us back in control of our lives.

GETTING STARTED

There are two forms of practising mindfulness – formal and informal. Formal practice involves different methods of mindful meditation, such as concentrating on breath, that are done for specific periods of time, say thirty minutes at a time, to formally engage mindfulness practice. These train the body and brain to concentrate on the moment. Later in the book there is a series of guided mindfulness meditations for you to follow.

A good way to start, though, is with more informal mindfulness. This refers to taking small moments – as short as a few seconds – throughout the day, to fully pay attention to what is happening at that moment, be it when you are eating, having a shower, hanging up washing, playing with a child or receiving a telephone call. Did you really taste the food, feel the textures of the clothes, concentrate on the child or listen to what the person at the other end of the phone was saying? Consider the activities in which you often find yourself daydreaming or mindlessly thinking of something else. These moments provide us with the opportunity to practise mindfulness.

Here is how to start:

❋ Begin by bringing your attention to the feelings in your body

❋ Breathe through your nose, allowing your lungs to fill and your abdomen to expand fully

❋ Now breathe out of your mouth and notice where you feel the breath the most

❋ Start your task slowly and with each breath feel yourself slowing down and becoming more immersed in the moment

❋ Engage your senses and notice every sight, touch and sound

❋ If your mind wanders, try to gently bring it back to focus on your breathing and senses

❋ Allow yourself to bask in the comfort of the present moment

HOW MINDFULNESS BEGAN

The M Word – where did it come from? Like most mind-body therapies, mindfulness isn't new. Its roots lie in ancient Buddhism and mindfulness is at the core of Buddhist meditation. The secular form of mindfulness, which is what most of us today are thinking of, was popularised by scientist, writer and meditation teacher Jon Kabat-Zinn, who started a stress-reduction clinic at the University of Massachusetts Medical School in the 1970s, with the idea of bringing Buddhist meditation into the mainstream of medicine. His definition of mindfulness is 'paying attention on purpose, in the present moment and non-judgementally, to the unfolding of experience, moment to moment'.

In 1979, Kabat-Zinn developed an eight-week programme called Mindfulness-Based Stress Reduction (MBSR) and wrote a book about his findings and research, full of success stories about how mindfulness can help with a range of problems from stress and anxiety to dealing with time pressures. This MBSR programme is now offered in over 200 medical centres, hospitals and clinics around the world and since its inception has been completed by more than 20,000 people.

In the 1990s, a trio of scientists further developed a practice called Mindfulness-Based Cognitive Therapy (MBCT) to help people suffering from depression. MCBT is now approved in the UK by the National Institute of Clinical Excellence (NICE) as a treatment choice to help prevent relapse in depression and the after-effects of trauma.

Since then a huge body of research around the world has demonstrated how mindfulness-based interventions improve mental and physical health and could be key to fighting disease and combatting recurrent stress-related conditions. Mindfulness has migrated to schools, into workplaces, prisons, the military and high-level sports. However it is practised, mindfulness is a strong antidote to the stresses of twenty-first-century society, where our lives are saturated with digital technology and the urge to do more and more in less time.

THE AMAZING BENEFITS OF PRACTISING MINDFULNESS

MINDFULNESS IMPROVES WELL-BEING

- Allows you to become fully absorbed in the moment, making it easier to enjoy pleasures as they occur
- Creates greater capacity to deal with stressful events
- Contributes to the feeling of being content with life
- Makes you better able to form closer relationships with others and be more compassionate
- Reduces worries about the future or regrets about the past
- Allows you to see situations more clearly
- Improves marital quality and communication
- Boosts working memory, attention span and focus

MINDFULNESS IMPROVES PHYSICAL HEALTH

✳ Reduces stress and is linked with decreased levels of the stress hormone cortisol

✳ Lowers blood pressure

✳ Helps to relieve chronic pain

✳ Makes you sleep better

✳ Strengthens your immune system to fight off infections

✳ Is considered an excellent strategy for weight loss

✳ Can help with symptoms of certain physical conditions, such as heart disease, irritable bowel syndrome, cancer and HIV

MINDFULNESS IMPROVES MENTAL HEALTH

✳ Helps to relieve stress, anxiety and depression

✳ Lowers risk of depression

✳ Helps to treat eating disorders

✳ Enhances creativity

✳ Can help when combating substance abuse

✳ Reduces feeling of loneliness

MINDFULNESS
CAN CHANGE OUR BRAINS!

As the popularity of mindfulness grows, brain imaging techniques are showing that this ancient practice can profoundly change the way different regions of the brain communicate with each other, as well as actually change the structure of the brain itself. One of the key areas of the brain involved in happiness is the left prefrontal cortex. Activity in this area increases when you are smiling at someone, concentrating on your favourite music or thinking about something you love. In contrast the right side of the frontal lobe – the right prefrontal cortex – is more active when people feel sad.

Matthieu Ricard, a French-born biologist turned Buddhist monk, has been hailed by scientists as the most upbeat person in the world. He earned the title when a scan of his brain showed the highest-yet recorded activity in the area associated with positive emotions – they were so high that the research team thought the scanner was malfunctioning! Mindfulness meditation strengthens the activity in the left prefrontal cortex (the 'happiness' side) and reduces activity in the right prefrontal cortex, the 'sadness' side.

Ricard argues that we can develop our potential for happiness, calm and a state of inner fulfilment. He says: 'The basic root of happiness lies in our minds; outer circumstances are nothing more than adverse or favourable.'

A HANDFUL OF MINDFULNESS EXERCISES TO TRY

IF YOU HAVE ONE MINUTE: MINDFUL SQUARE BREATHING

In our busy lives, as our minds are constantly pulled from one place to the next, leaving us anxious and apprehensive, one of the best ways we can practise mindfulness is to focus on our breathing.

This exercise can be done anywhere, at any time. All you have to do is focus on your breath for sixty seconds.

Start by breathing in and out slowly and purposefully, then introduce the four simple breath segments below. All should be done to the count of four.

❋ Inhale 2 3 4

❋ Hold 2 3 4

❋ Exhale 2 3 4

❋ Hold 2 3 4

❋ Repeat

Whenever your mind wanders, bring your focus back to your breath and the sensation of breathing in and expanding your lungs.

If you would like to give your mind something extra to focus on, use a four-sided object, preferably a square, as a visual guide. This can be something like a window, a picture frame or a child's building block. Start in the upper left-hand corner. As you inhale move your gaze to the upper right-hand corner. As you hold your breath, move your gaze to the lower right-hand corner. Exhale and move your eyes to the lower right-hand corner. Finally, as you complete the cycle and hold again, bring your eyes to the upper left-hand corner. Repeat.

IF YOU HAVE FIVE MINUTES:
MINDFUL LISTENING

This exercise is designed to help you listen in a non-judgemental way. When we hear sounds, much of what our brain processes is influenced by thoughts of past experiences, while many environmental noises around us barely register in our awareness. Listening to music in all its complexities and layers is a powerful way to help us slow down and really experience the present moment.

❋ Select a piece of music from your music collection, perhaps a relaxing classical piece or something by an artist you particularly love, or a song that has a special meaning for you.

❋ Find a comfortable place where you can be undisturbed for five minutes. Put on headphones if there is too much noise around you.

❋ Start by taking a few relaxing deep breaths. Focus on the sensations in your body.

❋ Try to become fully entwined with the music and the sounds that are being played or sung. Let your awareness climb inside the track and along the sound waves. Observe the speed, the melody, the sound of each instrument.

 If you find your attention wandering and that you're having thoughts, such as memories or things that need to be done, let go of them and gently bring your focus back to the sounds and sensations of the music.

IF YOU HAVE TWENTY MINUTES:
BODY-SCAN EXERCISE

This exercise helps to increase mind-body awareness, release tension and quieten the mind.

To do the exercise you may want to sit in a chair, or to lie on the floor and rest your head on a cushion or pillow. Make sure you will not be disturbed: shut the door and switch off your phone. It is best to wear loose and comfortable clothes. Make sure you're warm enough.

❋ First, take a few moments to check in with your body. Notice the sensations that are present, such as the contact your body is making with the chair or the floor. Feel the weight and density of your body.

❋ Bring your attention to the natural flow of your breath. Note how your abdomen gently rises as you inhale and falls as you exhale. On each out-breath, let your body sink deeper into the chair or the floor. Feel the breath as it enters your nostrils, feeling your lungs expand and the slight pause between the inhalation and the exhalation.

❋ If you feel emotions, accept them and move on. Remember the intention of this practice is not to feel a certain way. It is just, as best you can, to bring awareness to any sensations you detect, as you focus on each part of your body in turn.

✳ Start by focusing on the crown of your head. How does it feel? Is there any tingling, numbness or tightness? Just become aware, do not try to change any feelings. Then move down to your forehead, noticing any sensations. Can you feel your pulse in your forehead?

✳ Then bring your attention to the eyes, nose, cheeks, mouth, jaw, tongue, chin, neck and finally the ears. Feel the changing sensations from moment to moment, such as the the sounds coming into your ears or the sensation of air in your throat.

✳ Then, letting go of the head and face, move your awareness into the neck and shoulders. Notice these strong muscles and any tension you might be holding here. Feel the parts of your body that are in contact with the floor and stretch your awareness into them – arms, elbows, wrists, hands and fingers. Notice any feelings.

✳ Shift the focus now to the front of the body, the chest area. Notice the subtle rise and fall of the chest with the in- and out-breath, turning your awareness to the ribcage. Can you feel your own heartbeat?

✳ Turn your awareness now to the abdomen and stomach, the place where we feel our 'gut feelings', noticing any feelings and accepting them.

✳ Then focus on the back of your body and your spine. Scan down from your shoulder blades to the middle of your back and then your lower back, before moving your awareness to the pelvis area, the hip bones, sitting bones and groin.

✳ From time to time check you are fully focused; if you are starting to daydream or have other thoughts, slowly bring your attention back to the part of the body you are concentrating on.

✳ Now let go of the torso as the centre of your awareness and move your attention into the thighs of both legs, feeling the weight of your legs, gently noticing what other sensations there are here.

✳ Turn your attention towards the knees and into the calves of both legs. Finally move your attention into both feet: the arches, the heels, the balls and the tops of the feet. Notice how your feet feel as they touch the floor. Bring your attention to the toes. What temperature are they? Is there any tingling?

✳ Now, taking one or two deep breaths, widen your focus to take in the whole body. Be fully present and aware of your entire body and feel the breath flowing freely in and out of your system. Allow yourself to feel completely relaxed, yet maintain your full attention to the moment.

- When you feel ready, slowly begin to wriggle your toes and fingers. Slowly open your eyes and stretch gently. Enjoy the feeling of calm and being fully connected with the present moment.

WHAT MAKES ME FEEL CALM?

Curling up on the sofa with a new hardback book, tuning in to fascinating programmes on Radio 4, eating a juicy mango in the bath, discovering new music, lighting a delicious scented candle . . . Calm can come in many forms.

List the things that make you feel calm.

....

....

....

....

....

....

....

....

....

....

....

....

....

....

....

INCREASING GRATITUDE

Feeling grateful for what we have is something we all know we need to acknowledge a bit more often. Day to day, rather than thinking about what we love about our lives, we find ourselves striving for something more and obsessing about what we don't have: material items, body shapes, perfect relationships, working lives and so on. Like many women, I tend to think a new wardrobe, being a stone lighter and living in a bigger house will be the answer to everything. But is that true?

Although we do find satisfaction from striving for the things we covet, scientific research has proved that, on the other side, feelings of insufficiency and imperfection will hold us back and are barriers to feeling happy and calm. Research shows that gratitude has powerful effects on physical health, self-worth and personal relationships. Regular appreciation, whether it's for the big things in life like having healthy children and good friends, or on a smaller scale, like receiving a nice email or the sun shining, boosts feelings of optimism. Like being mindful, showing gratitude also fosters the resilience needed to deal with life's obstacles.

Professor Robert Emmons, the world's leading scientific researcher on gratitude, has overseen decades of studies on the subject and has proved that gratitude improves both psychological and physical health. People who practise gratitude feel happier, more optimistic and more joyous more often. They have stronger relationships, have higher self-esteem, are more compassionate and are less likely to suffer from mental illnesses like depression. In addition, they have stronger immune systems, sleep better, are fitter, report fewer physical aches and are more likely to visit the doctor, which may lead to living longer lives.

Professor Emmons and other experts on the subject explain that appreciating everyday experiences and interactions is the first level of gratitude, but moving on from that, a second layer is still being able to appreciate what we have after a major disappointment or loss. This helps us pave the way for new understandings, relationships and connections.

WRITE A JOURNAL OR PEN A LETTER . . .

As part of your journey towards a calmer life, there are various ways you can increase feelings of gratitude, such as keeping a journal.

At the end of every day, write down three to five things that went well and the things you are grateful for; these can be small things like your train arriving on time, or having a pleasant exchange with a neighbour.

Another lovely idea is to write thank-you notes. Pen a letter or email to someone in your life to thank them for something. According to Professor Emmons, people who do this report an improvement in both symptoms of depression and physical aches and pains, even if they don't send the letters. He says: 'Something happens when we put our feelings into words. Our brains begin to change.'

MAKE . . . A GRATITUDE JAR

This idea is great for mums. Time seems to barrel past in a blur – do you really remember the small things that happened? What was great about last Wednesday? A random Monday last month? Encourage the whole family to take part; there are no rules and, by committing to making a Gratitude Jar, you are halfway to feeling happier.

* Find an old jar – any size from jam jar upwards will do.

* Take a piece of paper and jot down something you are grateful for – it can be anything, from a burst of emotion to a random act of kindness – and the date.

* Repeat as regularly as you wish, but aim for at least one note every few days.

* Periodically open the jar and read the notes and the memories will come flooding back: personal triumphs, cosy Sundays, delicious meals round the table, laughter, a moment of joy . . .

'Begin doing what you want to do now. We are not living in eternity. We only have this moment, sparkling like a star in our hand and melting like a snowflake.'

FRANCIS BACON

BALANCE YOUR COMPLAINTS

From tiredness to bad weather, we all complain in our daily lives. It is a useful exercise to write down each grumble for a day or even a week. Keep a piece of paper or pen in your pocket or make notes on your phone and, each time you find yourself complaining, note down your gripe.

At the end of each day, look at your list and match each complaint with something you are grateful for or happy about, however small – a great cup of tea or a shared joke. Do this at a regular time each day, like bedtime or when you brush your teeth; studies show that it is easier to stick to a new habit if you link it to something you already do.

This exercise will start to change your mindset and help you focus on the positives. The more you appreciate the good things, the more you increase your capacity to notice them.

The Guest House

RUMI

This being human is a guest house.
Every morning a new arrival.

A joy, a depression, a meanness,
some momentary awareness comes
as an unexpected visitor.

Welcome and entertain them all!
Even if they're a crowd of sorrows,
who violently sweep your house
empty of its furniture,
still, treat each guest honourably.
He may be clearing you out
for some new delight.

The dark thought, the shame, the malice,
meet them at the door laughing,
and invite them in.

Be grateful for whoever comes,
because each has been sent
as a guide from beyond.

CHAPTER 2

NOURISH

'To keep the body in
good health is a duty ...
otherwise we shall not
be able to keep our
mind strong and clear.'

BUDDHA

You are at a computer facing a barrage of emails and you type quickly, press reply, then grab the bulging sandwich that has been sitting on your desk. Before you've even registered eating it, you've finished and need to get on with the next bunch of emails.

Or the kids are in bed and you collapse on the sofa with a plate of pasta in your lap and shovel it in while watching the TV, without ever tasting it. Sound familiar?

There is a growing body of research showing that slower, more mindful eating could not only help us shift unwanted weight but could also steer us towards healthier food choices. It has also been proven to help reduce anxious thoughts about food and our bodies.

You may have a complicated relationship with food and perhaps find yourself overeating to cope with your emotions; mindful eating can help you learn to cope better and no longer manage your feelings through comfort eating. Recent research published in the journal *Complementary Therapies in Medicine* showed that after six weeks of mindfulness training, participants experienced a 16 per cent decrease in out-of-control eating, a 39 per cent decrease in hunger and a 43 per cent decrease in binge-eating incidences.

According to scientists, digestion involves a complex series of hormonal signals between the stomach and the nervous system and it takes about twenty minutes for the brain to register satiety. Therefore, if you eat while you are distracted by other activities such as typing, driving or watching television, you may overeat beyond the point of fullness. Also, it is thought that if we eat when we are stressed the body does not digest the food in the same way and so we do not derive the same full nutritional value from it as we would from a meal eaten calmly.

Mindful eating helps us learn to hear what our body is telling us about hunger and satisfaction. In our society, where food is so readily available, portions are large and there are so many fad diets claiming to help, mindful eating plugs us back in to our body's cues. We learn to pay attention to the experience of eating and drinking and the colours, textures, flavours and smell of the food we are eating. Experts say that people who eat mindfully report increased enjoyment of food, improved digestion and are satisfied with less. Here are a few tips to help you start eating more mindfully:

❋ Savour each bite. Mindfulness means really paying attention to what you are eating. Think about the texture and flavour of the food and slow down. Take time to chew each mouthful, put down your fork between bites and, if you have young children, turn it into a game – see who can chew their food for longest. Or try something different and force yourself to slow down; you could switch hands or try to eat with chopsticks.

❋ Don't eat in front of the television, and remove your phone from the table. When we are distracted we cannot focus on what we are eating. A review of twenty-five studies on the subject at the University of Liverpool in 2013 found that when eating in front of the television, we eat 10 per cent more on average and consume more than 25 per cent extra at a later meal. If we sit at the table without diversions, it is easier to be mindful of what is on our plates.

❋ Get to know what you are eating better. Do you ever stop to think about where the food you are eating comes from? If you take time to understand more about the origins of the food you eat, you will gain a deeper appreciation for it and this might help to change your eating habits.

✳ Working harder for your food means you eat less. That's what one study at Eastern Illinois University found when they gave two groups of participants pistachio nuts. They gave one group nuts that had already been shelled and the other group had to de-shell them. The former group consumed 211 calories on average, while the latter only ate 125 calories; but both groups rated their feelings of satisfaction and fullness the same.

✳ Keep a food diary and write down everything you eat and why you ate it – was it because you were hungry? Or were you tired, bored or stressed? By becoming more aware of our emotional eating triggers and patterns, we can more easily adjust them and make healthy changes.

EAT A SQUARE OF CHOCOLATE MINDFULLY

Before you pick up the chocolate, take a few deep breaths in through your nose and out through your mouth, allowing your body and mind to relax. Forget about anything you have been doing and turn your attention fully to the chocolate.

Firstly, consider the wrapped chocolate – what does it say on the packaging and where does it come from? Try to think about the journey the chocolate has been on to be delivered into your hands. Pick it up and open the wrapper. Does it make a sound? Do you feel a sense of urgency or anticipation, or guilt and unease? Break a piece of chocolate off. Does it make a sound?

Take the piece and look at it closely. Consider its colour, texture and weight. What does it smell like and what do you feel like when you smell it? Does it feel smooth between your fingers?

Put the chocolate in your mouth but do not chew or crunch it. Let it melt slowly and notice where in your mouth you taste it. What is the flavour? Move the chocolate around your mouth with your tongue and think about what is happening in each area of your mouth: teeth, tongue and lips. Does the taste change?

Swallow the chocolate, focusing on the sensation. Is there an aftertaste that lingers? How do you feel physically and emotionally? Sit for a minute and think about the experience. Do your senses feel more alive?

THE FAMILY THAT EATS TOGETHER, STAYS TOGETHER

What's the most important thing a family can do together? Eat together, say researchers. Eating together is a chance to recharge, tell stories, fill each other in about your respective days and laugh.

Over the past fifteen years, scientists have shown that sharing a family meal is good for the spirit, for our health and for our relationships. Studies link regular family meals with lower rates of depression, higher grades in education and increased levels of self-esteem. Research also indicates that dinner conversation is a more powerful language booster for young children than reading. Having regular meals at home also lowers the rates of obesity because foods eaten at home are more likely to include nutrient-rich food from all food groups and contain less sugar and fat.

It can be challenging to incorporate mindfulness into a social situation, but try talking about the food you are eating – what you like about it, where it has come from and the flavours and textures.

NOURISHING FOODS TO FIGHT STRESS

It's no surprise that when we eat well, we feel well. When we're busy with children, work and rushing around after everyone else, it can be hard to plan healthy meals and snacks. However, some foods have properties that make us feel calmer.

Avocado: They are rich in B vitamins, which are key for healthy nerves and brain cells and play an important role in producing brain chemicals that affect our mood and other brain functions. They are also high in monounsaturated fat, which can improve cholesterol levels and decrease the risk of heart disease. Mash avocado on toast or add it to salads.

Blueberries: Rich in antioxidants and stress-fighting Vitamin C, blueberries offer a low-calorie and high-fibre fruit option. For a delicious snack, add to a smoothie or fruit salad.

Spinach: Rich in magnesium, spinach and other leafy greens help to fight indigestion, fatigue and stress. Add spinach to salads, steam as a side dish or add some to a home-made soup or smoothie.

Asparagus: Low mood and depression is linked to low levels of folic acid and one single cup of asparagus provides two thirds of your daily needs. Folic acid helps to maintain steady mood and aids the body in producing serotonin, a chemical that makes us feel happy. Cook some asparagus tips as a side dish, or add to an omelette.

Cottage Cheese: This is high in protein and calcium and will keep you fuller for longer, rather than causing your blood sugar to spike and then crash. Calcium helps relax and strengthen the nervous system for better management of stress. Spread cottage cheese on crackers, add to a jacket potato or make pancakes.

Almonds: A good source of Vitamins B2 (fantastic for energy) and E (which has antioxidant properties), almonds also contain magnesium and zinc which are great for nerve and immune function respectively. Munch on some between meals or spread almond butter on fruit slices.

Oranges: Packed with Vitamin C, which is known for lowering levels of the stress hormone cortisol, oranges are also high in Vitamin A, which is good for skin. Simply eat a whole orange, or enjoy a freshly squeezed orange juice with breakfast.

Salmon: Salmon and other oily fish is an excellent source of

Omega 3 fatty acids, which can help balance stress hormones, tame mood swings and fight heart disease. In a study at Oregon State University, medical students who took Omega 3 supplements reported a 20 per cent reduction in anxiety compared to the group given placebo pills. Serve grilled or poached or in a curry, salad or pasta dish.

Dark chocolate: While it is important not to overindulge, chocoholics will be pleased to know that research has shown that eating dark chocolate can help to reduce stress levels; and it is also full of antioxidants. Choose varieties with 70 per cent cocoa and satisfy your sweet tooth by enjoying the odd square.

Milk: Milk is not only an excellent source of calcium but is also packed with Vitamin D, which is thought to boost happiness. A fifty-year-long study at London's UCL Institute of Child Health found an association between reduced levels of Vitamin D and an increased risk of depression and anxiety.

Seeds: Pumpkin seeds, sunflower seeds and flaxseeds are all excellent sources of magnesium, which helps to regulate emotions. Sprinkle over porridge or salads, add to soups or make a roasted seed and nut mix for snacks.

MAKE . . . SUPERFOOD OVERNIGHT OATS

It can be hard to find time for breakfast but there is a reason it is called the most important meal of the day. When you are trying to keep your energy levels high while staying calm and relaxed, one of the most important things to remember is never to skip meals. After about five hours without food hunger will start to overwhelm the senses, leading to bad food choices such as hitting the nearest vending machine. The stress hormone cortisol causes food cravings and women in particular tend to crave carbs, especially sweet foods, according to researchers at the University of California.

Overnight oats are the perfect food for busy mornings. They can be made the night before and are loaded with lots of different superfoods for the ultimate healthy breakfast.

INGREDIENTS:

1 cup unsweetened almond milk
1 cup rolled oats
1 banana
1 cup Greek yogurt
2 tbsp chia seeds
1 tbsp dried goji berries

handful of pumpkin seeds
2 handfuls of raspberries
sprinkle of shredded coconut

DIRECTIONS:

Put a small amount of almond milk in a bowl or large cup and layer one part milk to one part oats, to one part yogurt, one part banana and a small sprinkling of chia seeds and dried goji berries, in whatever order you wish. Chia seeds will help thicken the texture and consistency. They are also an excellent source of fibre, Omega 3 fatty acids and protein.

Refrigerate for at least five hours or overnight. In the morning, add the pumpkin seeds, raspberries and coconut and any additional milk to the consistency you prefer. You can mix in any other ingredients you like, such as different fresh or dried fruit, spices, seeds, protein powder and granola.

As well as a delicious breakfast, overnight oats make a great snack when you are in a rush.

'One cannot think well,
love well, sleep well, if
one has not dined well.'

A ROOM OF ONE'S OWN, VIRGINIA WOOLF

A LETTER . . . TO MY BODY

Most of us have a complicated relationship with our body and food; more often than not, we want to change something about our legs /stomachs/ upper arms and find ourselves battling with our diet. What we don't do nearly enough is think about which parts of our bodies we love and why. Writing this down might feel a bit strange at first but this can be a powerful exercise.

For guidance I would consider thinking about a part of your body that's been injured and healed well. Tell it how grateful/ impressed you are? Or think of how your legs are strong enough for you to go on restorative walks and how much you appreciate that. Or indeed the last time someone paid your body a compliment.

Dear Body,:

CREATE YOUR OWN TEA RITUAL

'Would you like an
adventure now, or shall
we have our tea first?'

PETER PAN, J.M. BARRIE

Having a cup of tea is always an enjoyable break in a busy day, but by creating a ritual around it, you can give yourself time to more mindfully enjoy a moment of quiet and relaxation.

In cultures around the world, tea and its preparation and consumption is a high art and a prized part of a healthy diet. For example, the Japanese tea ceremony, also called the Way of Tea (Chado) and influenced by Zen Buddhism, involves the ceremonial, ritualistic presentation and preparation of matcha, a powdered green tea, while in Tibet, they love nothing more than mixing their tea with yak butter and salt to create a high-fat and energy-boosting

drink to deal with life at the high altitudes of the
Himalayas.

The culture of tea-drinking reached Europe from China in the
seventeenth century when Portuguese and Dutch traders
brought tea leaves back along with silks and spices, mainly
out of curiosity. Diarist Samuel Pepys mentions having his first
cup of tea in an entry from 1660, saying: 'And afterwards I did
send for a cup of tea (a China drink) of which I had never
drunk before.'

Nowadays we in the UK drink 165 million cups a day and
there are a huge number of varieties, including a myriad of
herbal, flower and fruit options as well as black, white and
green teas.

Tea has long been associated with mental health benefits
such as improved attention, mental clarity and relaxation.
Making a simple cuppa also offers a wonderful opportunity to
stop and be mindful. Buddhist monk Thich Nhat Hanh says:
'Drink your tea slowly and reverently, as if it is the axis on
which the world earth revolves – slowly, evenly, without
rushing toward the future; live the actual moment. Only this
moment is life.'

'The tea ritual: such a precise repetition of the same gestures and the same tastes; accession to simple, authentic and refined sensations, a license given to all, at little cost, to become aristocrats of taste, because tea is the beverage of the wealthy and the poor; the tea ritual, therefore, has the extraordinary virtue of introducing into the absurdity of our lives an aperture of serene harmony. Yes, the world may aspire to vacuousness, lost souls mourn beauty, insignificance surrounds us. Then let us drink a cup of tea. Silence descends, one hears the wind outside, autumn leaves rustle and take flight, the cat sleeps in a warm pool of light. And, with each swallow, time is sublimed.'

MURIEL BARBERY,
THE ELEGANCE OF THE HEDGEHOG

CHAPTER 3

SLEEP

'Sleep is the best meditation.'

DALAI LAMA

'll be up in a minute!' How often do you find yourself saying that? Then after writing that final email, sorting tomorrow's lunches, maybe doing some laundry or watching that extra episode of your favourite box set you finally turn in for the day. With our lives busier than ever, sleep is being pushed further and further down the priority list. Most of us view sleep as an optional luxury – we think we can 'grab some later' or 'catch up' at a better time but the reality is that, just like eating, we must make time for it and there are no shortcuts.

On average we sleep two hours less than we did in 1960, and one recent survey of 20,000 people showed that women are getting an average of just five hours a night. While some people need more sleep than others, experts agree that we all need between six and nine hours per night. And if you ever needed an excuse to make your husband or partner get up with the children, it has also been scientifically proven that women need more sleep than men!

Sleep problems affect one in three of us at any one time, and ten per cent of the country suffers from chronic insomnia. Combined with some mums being woken up regularly by small children, and our general sleep debt, the result is that our day-to-day lives are affected, as well as our long-term physical and mental health. In the long term, poor sleep has been found to increase the risk of various serious illnesses, including Type 2 diabetes, obesity, anxiety and depression, stroke, hypertension and cardiovascular disease. We also get ill more often because lack of sleep alters immune function, including the activity of the so-called killer cells, which fight off infection and see off potential threats.

On a day-to-day basis, sleep debt has consequences for our mood and may make us irritable, impatient or unable to concentrate clearly. Sleep deprivation affects the brain function, especially those functions associated with the frontal lobe, interfering with high-level cognitive processes called executive functions. This can undermine judgement, critical thinking, planning, organisation, problem-solving and relationships.

Lack of sleep is also said to profoundly affect memory and performance; people who sleep less than seven hours a night have reaction times similar to people who have been completely deprived of sleep for one or two nights.

Sleep is one of the most important tools when it comes to fighting anxiety and stress. Research in 2005 concluded that insomnia often goes hand in hand with depression and anxiety and increases the risk of developing a mood disorder. Studies point to the fact that those who are prone to anxiety and also sleep deprived often have noteworthy brain dysfunctions that can cause further anxiety.

Why this happens is not exactly clear, but it is believed that when we sleep our brains regenerate neurons that influence various areas of thought and emotion. If you do not rest and these neurons do not regenerate – or, in some cases, stop firing altogether – you may be less able to cope. The brain then experiences more generic stress from working hard to compensate for the parts of the brain that have shut down.

Ever had a bad night and feel yourself reaching for the biscuit tin more often the next day? If you are struggling to keep your weight down and do not get enough sleep, this will not help! Sleep helps to maintain a healthy balance of the hormone ghrelin, which makes you feel hungry, and leptin, the chemical that makes you feel full. When you're not rested your levels of ghrelin elevate and your levels of leptin drop. Research has also shown that sleep-deprived brains respond differently to high-calorie foods and the body metabolises those foods less effectively. Studies have shown that people who sleep less than seven hours a night are 30 per cent more likely to be obese than those who get nine hours' shut-eye. Ongoing studies are looking at whether adequate sleep should be part of standard weight-loss programmes.

Sleep is as powerful as diet and exercise when it comes to living a longer life. One study published in the *European Journal of Preventive Cardiology* revealed that more than seven hours of sleep a night enhanced the benefits of a healthy lifestyle. People who exercised, ate a healthy diet, didn't smoke and drank in moderation had a 67 per cent lower risk of dying from heart disease. But for those who also had sufficient sleep, the risk was 83 per cent lower. That's a pretty powerful argument for hitting the sack . . .

While you probably know how important it is to get adequate sleep, the scary thing is that, if you are chronically sleep deprived, you may not realise it. While some people claim they can get by on as little as four hours per night, most of us do not belong to this exclusive little club; experts suggest that only one to three per cent of the population can function properly in this way. After a long period of sleep deprivation (like having small children) you begin to fail to register how tired you really are. Deep down you probably know that you are exhausted, but there may seem no way to rectify the issue so you continue to not priortise sleep or recognise its significance.

TEN BRILLIANT TIPS FOR A BLISSFUL NIGHT'S REST

✳ Naturally regulate your sleep–awake cycle: Do you remember when you first brought your newborn baby home and you had to help them learn about day and night? Melatonin is a naturally occurring hormone controlled by light exposure that helps to regulate your sleep–awake cycle. At night time when it's dark, your brain should secrete more melatonin, making you sleepy, and during the day it should secrete less so you feel alert. During the day, try to increase your exposure to natural light, take regular breaks in the fresh air and keep the blinds or curtains open. At least an hour before bedtime, put your phone or tablet away and turn off the television; the light suppresses melatonin production. Make sure the room is dark or use an eye mask.

✳ Create a relaxing bedtime atmosphere: Most people sleep best when the room is cool – between 16 and 18 degrees, with adequate ventilation. Try to keep noise to a minimum or invest in decent earplugs to block out unwanted noise. Research shows that sleeping in an uncomfortable bed could rob you of an hour's sleep per night, so invest in a comfortable bed and good pillows.

※ Only use your bed for sleeping and sex: This way, when you lie down in bed your body receives a powerful cue that it's time to sleep. Never, for example, watch television in bed.

※ Stay away from big meals: Eat your main evening meal at least two hours before you go to bed; otherwise you may overload your digestive system and experience bloating, which makes it difficult to sleep.

※ Exercise regularly: You don't need to be sprinting round the block every day, but twenty to thirty minutes daily of exercise that raises your heart rate is a good target to aim for. If you have young children, a brisk walk with the buggy is ideal. Cycling or vigorous housework also count. Aim to finish any vigorous exercise three to four hours before going to bed.

※ Stick to a sleep schedule: Try to keep regular hours, so you go to bed and wake up at the same time every day. This helps to regulate your body clock.

※ Look for hidden caffeine: A cup (or three!) of coffee is fine in the morning but try to limit your caffeine intake after midday. Even the small amounts of caffeine found in chocolate may affect your sleep.

❋ Wear some socks: Swiss researchers found that wearing bed socks helps us go to sleep in half the normal time. When we are about to drop off, the body redirects blood flow to our hands and feet; if they are warm, blood vessels can dilate and allow for greater blood flow, which helps us nod off.

❋ Limit your alcohol intake: While a nightcap might seem like a good idea and alcohol can initially make you fall asleep faster, it causes a lot of brain arousal once it's metabolised, meaning you will wake up more during the night.

❋ Change your sleep mindset: Nothing aggravates sleeplessness more than worrying about it. The more pressure you put on yourself to sleep, the less likely it is that you will drop off. Focus instead on the idea of getting rest – and you may be surprised at how quickly you nod off.

MAKE . . . A SWEET DREAMS BANANA AND KIWI SMOOTHIE

If you want a snack before turning in, try a banana and kiwi smoothie, packed with Vitamin D and calcium. According to a study in the *Journal of Sleep Research*, these two nutrients are associated with decreased odds of having problems staying and falling asleep – 17 and 16 per cent, respectively. Bananas are also a great source of magnesium and B6, which both help your body to make serotonin, a chemical messenger that's believed to act as a mood stabiliser. Researchers in Taiwan have also linked kiwi to substantial improvements in both sleep quality and quantity due to its high antioxidant and serotonin levels.

INGREDIENTS:

1 cup milk (use a non-dairy substitute if you need to)
1 kiwi
1 fresh banana
¼ tsp nutmeg
1 tsp honey

DIRECTIONS:

Put all the ingredients into a blender and blend for around thirty seconds.

HOW TO ENJOY THE PERFECT SIESTA

Ahh, the nap. The domain of babies, children and the elderly, right? Wrong.

From boosting memory, alertness and creativity to increasing awareness, a little shut-eye can really help if you are tired. A nap can be particularly beneficial after a poor night's sleep and one recent study published in the Endocrine Society's *Journal of Clinical Endocrinology and Metabolism* found that a short nap could reverse the negative health effects of a poor night's sleep, reduce stress and bolster the immune system. It's also been proven that a short sleep is better than coffee for memory and motor skills. So hit the sofa!

❊ Watch the time. The most beneficial naps are those
that are kept relatively short, so you only enter the
first two stages of sleep. Once you enter the third,
slow wave or deeper sleep, it is much harder to wake
up and you will feel much groggier afterwards. Ideally
keep your naps to twenty minutes; set your alarm to
wake you up before you can enter into deep sleep.

❊ Find a quiet and dark place to limit distractions. Use
earplugs, listen to white noise or put on an eye mask.

❊ Coordinate your caffeine and drink your coffee before
you nap. It takes twenty to thirty minutes for caffeine
to kick in, so if you drink it just before you nap, it'll be
kicking in just as you are waking up, when you need it.

❊ Plan your nap well. If you have a baby who naps
regularly, have twenty minutes to kill before the
school run or half an hour spare in your day, schedule
that time out to take a nap, so you know you have
something on the horizon to look forward to.

❊ Don't feel guilty for napping. Napping is both natural
and beneficial. Try not to worry about other things
you need to do but just take deep, slow breaths and
let yourself drift off into the land of nod.

MAKE . . . YOUR OWN BEDTIME LAVENDER SCRUB

The skin is the largest organ, and a good scrub will stimulate blood circulation, drain lymph nodes and detoxify the body. Lavender essential oil brings its own benefits, including the ability to eliminate nervous tension and induce sleep. One recent study at Wesleyan University in the US asked 31 men and women to sniff lavender essential oil one night and then distilled water the next, for four two-minute periods just before bedtime. The researchers tracked their sleep with brain scans. On the night the participants smelled the lavender, they slept more soundly and also felt more energised the next day.

While an expensive body product is always a lovely treat, you can make your own calming lavender sugar scrub much more cheaply – and due to its simplicity, if you have small children at home, they can help. Having a shower or bath and using this scrub is a lovely pre-bedtime ritual.

INGREDIENTS:

2 cups granulated sugar – you can use brown or white
¼ cup olive, almond or coconut oil
5 to 8 drops lavender essential oil
1 tablespoon dried lavender (optional)
Few drops of purple food colouring (optional)

DIRECTIONS:

Pour the sugar into a bowl and slowly add the olive, almond or coconut oil, while stirring. You can add more or less to create the perfect consistency for you. Mix thoroughly. Stir in the lavender oil and dried lavender and then colour it with the food colouring, if using. Again, you can use a varying amount of lavender depending on how strong you like your scrub. It will last up to three months if stored in an airtight container.

Use the scrub before bedtime. Warm to hot water is ideal to soften the skin, so shower for five minutes to let the water run warm or relax in the bath first, before rubbing the scrub between your hands with some water. Then rub on your skin in upward or circular strokes and concentrate on tough areas like elbows, feet and knees. Maintain a gentle pressure. Rinse off and pat your skin dry rather than rubbing, to retain some moisture. Relax and allow the oil to be absorbed.

'Let her sleep, for when
she wakes, she will
move mountains.'

NAPOLEON BONAPARTE

FIVE YOGA POSES FOR SLEEP

STANDING FORWARD BEND

Have your feet hip-width apart and keep a slight bend in your knees as you bend forward from the hips. Place your hands or fingers on the floor and then walk them back to just in front of, or beside, your feet. Exhale. Hold the pose for a few seconds, relaxing and breathing into it. This will release tension in your back, legs and shoulders.

CHILD POSE

Kneel down on the floor with your bottom resting on your feet, then bend forwards, letting your hands stretch out in front of you. Exhale slowly and rest your torso on your thighs so that your forehead touches the floor. Stay in this pose for a couple of breathes. This releases tension from the back, shoulders and chest, lengthens and stretches the spine and helps to relieve stress and anxiety.

SEATED FORWARD BEND

This exercise is like the standing forward bend but done sitting down. It is said to calm the mind and reduce fatigue.

Sit on the floor with your legs stretched in front of you. As in the standing forward bend, keep a slight bend in your knees as you bend forward from the hips. Let your hands rest on the floor either side of your legs. If you feel strain in your back, bend your knees more or place a cushion or folded blanket on your thighs for your torso to rest on.

SUPINE SPINAL TWIST

Lie on your back with both arms resting on the floor at shoulder height and bring both knees to your chest, then carefully bring both knees down to the floor on one side, twisting your upper body. Stay there for thirty seconds or so and then bring both knees back to your chest before lowering them to the floor on the other side.

This gentle twist massages, stretches and tones the internal organs and is a good way to decompress.

CORPSE POSE

Normally done at the end of a yoga class, this is a resting pose,.

Lie on your back in a neutral position – arms alongside, but not touching, the body, with your palms facing upwards, and legs and feet slightly apart but relaxed. Let your body feel heavy and focus on your breath, stay here until you feel utterly relaxed.

'All that we see or
seem, is but a dream
within a dream.'

EDGAR ALLAN POE

WHAT DO OUR DREAMS MEAN?

Have you ever woken up after a dream, desperate to share it with somebody and draw out its meaning? Dreams can frighten us, rock us, inspire us and in some cases, motivate us. Scientists have debated the meaning and purpose of dreams for decades, and psychotherapists have long believed that our dreams give us insights into feelings and internal struggles of which we may not always be consciously aware.

It is hard not to believe that our nocturnal dreams carry some sort of significance, and thinking about how your dreams may relate to what is going on in your life can help you think about and understand your personal issues.

While there any many dream dictionaries out there to help harness the power and meaning of our dreams, many therapists believe them to be of limited use because they give universal meaning to certain symbols and situations; in reality these symbols might actually have a unique meaning for each person.

It can be useful to note your feelings after waking from a dream in a journal that you keep by your bed. Jot down, without censoring yourself, what feelings and emotions specific images in a dream brought up for you. From time to time, look back at your journal to see if there are any recurring themes or patterns in your dreams.

Japanese Lullaby

EUGENE FIELD

Sleep, little pigeon, and fold your wings,
Little blue pigeon with velvet eyes;
Sleep to the singing of mother-bird swinging
Swinging the nest where her little one lies.

Away out yonder I see a star,
Silvery star with a tinkling song;
To the soft dew falling I hear it calling
Calling and tinkling the night along.

In through the window a moonbeam comes,
Little gold moonbeam with misty wings;
All silently creeping, it asks, 'Is he sleeping
Sleeping and dreaming while mother sings?'

Up from the sea there floats the sob
Of the waves that are breaking upon the shore,
As though they were groaning in anguish, and moaning
Bemoaning the ship that shall come no more.

But sleep, little pigeon, and fold your wings,
Little blue pigeon with mournful eyes;
Am I not singing? – see, I am swinging
Swinging the nest where my darling lies.

CHAPTER 4

NATURE

*'Turn your face towards
the sun and the shadows
will fall behind you.'*

MAORI PROVERB

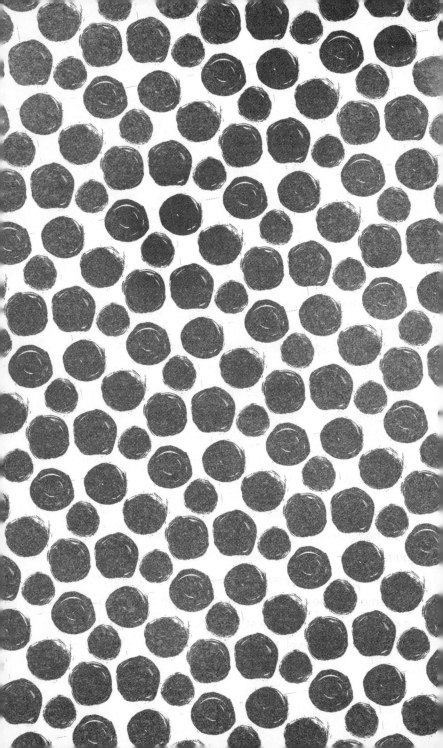

The dizzying, bare heights of Everest, the breathtaking ribbons of rainbow colour of the Northern Lights and the jaw-dropping, epic depths of the Grand Canyon are three of the natural wonders of the world. Yet in everyday nature too there are sights, sounds, textures and scents that are just as stunning and that connect us with stillness and inner peace. When was the last time you took time out to listen to the melodic thrum of rain against the windows, or to look at the rainbow colours of the leaves on the ground, or felt the firm pull of mud beneath your feet?

Lost in a world of phones, tablets and technology, many of us have become disconnected with nature. There is nothing quite like being deep in a forest with a canopy of trees sheltering us, the only sounds the wind, rustling trees, the movement of the creatures that call the wild home and our own breathing. Nature is a secret sanctuary and a shortcut to calm. On a basic level, being outside reminds us of the huge expanse of the universe in which we live and the unending cycle of the natural world; it gives us greater perspective and allows us to become more tranquil and centred.

The word nature is derived from the Latin word 'natura', meaning birth or character, while Mother Nature is a personification of nature that focuses on the life-giving and nurturing aspects of nature by embodying it in the form of a mother. Nature has a healing effect on the body. When you spend a few hours walking in the woods or camping by a lake, you breathe in fresh air and phytoncides, airborne compounds released by plants that experts say seem to boost our immune systems and lower blood pressure and stress levels.

There is clear scientific evidence that nature reduces stress and helps us find meaning and to connect with our inner selves. One recent large-scale study conducted by the University of Michigan, with partners from De Montfort University, the James Hutton Institute and Edge Hill University in the UK, found that group nature walks are linked with significantly lower incidences of depression, less perceived stress and enhanced mental health and well-being.

Another research project undertaken by Japanese scientists monitored the effects of nature mindfulness walks known as 'Shinrin-yoku', which literally means forest-bathing. Two groups of participants were sent walking: one group to the woods, and the other to the city. Afterwards, the scientists found that the participants who spent their day in the forest had 'lower concentrations of cortisol, lower pulse rates and lower blood pressure'. Put simply, they were less stressed.

Research has found that mental fatigue can be reduced and energy restored by going outdoors. One study even discovered that participants' mental energy bounced back when they simply looked at pictures of nature. Time outdoors also makes us more creative. In 2012 a study showed that people immersed in nature for four days – and disconnected from multimedia and technology – improved their performance on a creativity and problem-solving task by 50 per cent.

So next time you feel you need a boost or are feeling creatively bored or uninspired, look to nature, not your phone. Nature is a powerful remedy for when you are feeling overwhelmed.

WALK THIS WAY: HOW TO TAKE A MINDFUL WALK

Where will you walk today? Perhaps you need to go from A to B, or maybe you'll take a walk just for pleasure. On any given weekend in the UK, between seven and eight million people will go for a walk, travel from cities to walk in the open countryside or simply walk out of their front doors and keep going. Walking is one of the easiest ways to help develop mindfulness.

* Dress in comfortable clothes and shoes. Head to somewhere quiet, like a wood, park or walking path, and start walking. Stand straight with your back upright and try to distribute your weight evenly. Notice your posture. Do not plan where you are going, just start walking at a normal pace.

* As you walk, focus on your breathing. Think about which parts of your body move as you breathe in and out. Then turn your attention to the physical feelings in your body. What do your feet feel like as they connect with the ground? Are you swinging your arms gently?

✳ Then think about what you can hear: Are there birds tweeting in the nearby trees? Perhaps you are standing on leaves that make a satisfying crunching sound? Can you hear the wind? Be open to sounds as they happen, whether they are nearby or faraway. Do not seek them out or label them, just hear them.

✳ Now, think about what you can see. Take in all the images around you, from your own feet to the sky and everything around you. Look at the colours and the textures. What shades can you see?

✳ Finally, bring your awareness to what you can feel, such as the breeze against your skin. Pick up something natural, like a leaf or a stick. How does it feel in your hand? Think about the texture and temperature.

✳ If you find yourself losing concentration or your mind wandering, just gently guide your awareness back to the experience of walking.

✳ Take in the external environment and just breathe. Enjoy your journey.

'Study nature, love nature, stay close to nature. It will never fail you.'

FRANK LLOYD WRIGHT

I Wandered Lonely as a Cloud,

WILLIAM WORDSWORTH

I wandered lonely as a cloud
That floats on high o'er vales and hills,
When all at once I saw a crowd,
A host, of golden daffodils;
Beside the lake, beneath the trees,
Fluttering and dancing in the breeze.

Continuous as the stars that shine
And twinkle on the milky way,
They stretched in never-ending line
Along the margin of a bay:
Ten thousand saw I at a glance,
Tossing their heads in sprightly dance.

The waves beside them danced, but they
Out-did the sparkling leaves in glee;
A poet could not be but gay,
In such a jocund company!
I gazed – and gazed – but little thought
What wealth the show to me had brought:

For oft, when on my couch I lie
In vacant or in pensive mood,

They flash upon that inward eye
Which is the bliss of solitude;
And then my heart with pleasure fills,
And dances with the daffodils.

WAYS TO CONNECT WITH NATURE

As children, we are absorbed by nature; we jump in puddles and in the leaves, spend hours looking at creepy-crawlies and butterflies, roll in the grass and get covered from head to toe in mud. As we get older, we lose that fascination and spend less time connecting with nature. Here are some ideas about how to reconnect with and rediscover your enjoyment of the natural world, which can all be done alongside your children. Experiencing it with your children can remind you of your own long-ago fascination with the natural world:

* Walk barefoot outside and sink your feet into the grass

* 'Play in the dirt' by tending to a herb or vegetable garden, or make mud pies (whether you have young children or not!)

* On waking, open your blinds or window and really take in the scene in front of you – notice the colours of the sky, the shapes of the clouds, the sharp freshness of the air

* Bring nature indoors by buying houseplants or keeping a jar of fresh flowers in a room where you spend a lot of time

* Spend some time cloud-watching in the evening when sunset paints the sky orange, red and pink

* Press a flower

* Sleep in a tent outdoors

* Stargaze at night

* Have a picnic – whatever the time of year!

* Go wild swimming

* Borrow a dog and go walking

* Fly a kite

MAKE . . . A COURGETTE AND ALMOND LOAF CAKE

A cake with vegetables is a great way of indulging both yourself and your children, while also knowing that you are getting some natural goodness from your treats. Courgettes will add texture and flavour to this cake and keep it moist. It is easy to make and can be frozen for up to a month.

INGREDIENTS:

Butter for tin

75g soft brown sugar

2 large eggs

125ml vegetable oil

350g courgettes, grated coarsely

1 tsp vanilla extract

300g plain flour

2 tsp cinnamon

1 tsp nutmeg

½ tsp bicarbonate of soda

½ tsp baking powder

75g chopped almonds
100g sultanas

DIRECTIONS:

Heat the oven to 180°C (160 fan)/Gas 4. Butter a 2lb loaf tin and line it with baking parchment. In a bowl whisk the sugar, eggs and oil, then add the courgette and vanilla extract.

In a separate bowl, mix the flour and remaining ingredients together and add to the wet mixture. Pour into a tin and bake for one hour. Leave to cool and then serve.

MY FAVOURITE PLACES OUTDOORS

Whether it's sitting on a roof terrace in a city as the sun goes down, a seaside spot where we can watch the tide ebb and flow, or a rural space where we feel totally at peace, we all have outside places that we love to retreat to. List yours below.

....

....

....

....

....

....

....

....

....

....

....

....

....

....

....

....

....

LEAF DRAWING AND DOODLES

This is a great craft idea for all the family. It can be done at any time of year, although autumn does, of course, produce some spectacularly colourful leaves.

First head out and gather some leaves. Press them and dry them out for a few days in the sun. Then take some metallic marker pens and decorate them. Draw patterns, animals, faces . . . be as fun and creative as you can.

'Forget not that the earth delights to feel your bare feet and the winds long to play with your hair.'

KHALIL GIBRAN

CHAPTER 5

LOVE

'Love asks me no questions and gives me endless support.'

WILLIAM WORDSWORTH

We dream of having a relationship where we fall into our partner's arms at the end of the working day, delighted to see them, then sit round the table as a family with our children, laughing, chatting and enjoying each other's company. There is no baggage; there are no unrealistic ideals or misunderstandings. However, the reality is often more fraught than this. When a couple becomes a family, balancing working and busy lifestyles, many relationships, including those with our partner, extended families and closest friends, can suffer.

Being calm and mindful will have a positive impact on your relationships. A study in 2004 at the University of North Carolina showed that couples who practised mindfulness were happier in their relationships, were more accepting of one another and experienced less relationship stress and overall stress. A 2007 study backed this up and showed a correlation between mindfulness and quality of communication between romantic partners.

Even in the best relationships, some conflict is inevitable. We all fall into familiar ruts when it comes to disagreements and arguments. How often do you argue with those closest to you and say something you later regret? It is ironic how we lash out at the people we love the most.

However, when you practise mindfulness, you learn, when anger or another strong emotion bubbles inside you, to observe the emotions and thoughts without getting caught up in them. It becomes easier to maintain emotional balance and think about how to tackle the issue and respond in a calm and measured way. The emotions are still there; they are just not hijacked by familiar knee-jerk reactions. This means we can better understand our thoughts and emotions without becoming embroiled in intense reactions. Mindfulness can also help us regulate our emotions and calm our fears and anxieties before arguments can begin.

By being calm you really listen and hear when you are talking to others. This shows that you really care about what the other person has to say, as well as giving yourself the time and space to fully absorb what they are saying. It will also make you more empathetic, which will help you become more caring and compassionate and a better friend and partner.

Being more physically present makes for a better physical and sexual connection with your partner. Various studies have found that women who practise mindfulness report feeling more sexual arousal and more quickly. One study at Brown University in the US found that compared to the control group, women who had taken a 12-week meditation course were significantly faster at registering their body's responses to sexual stimuli, which are called 'interoceptive awareness'. The study's lead author argued that mindful sex involves being able to observe and describe what is happening inside your body, without labelling it as 'good' or 'bad' or trying to change feelings. They say that by being more mindful, you will be more present for the good moments and therefore reap more happiness and fun from sex with your partner.

LOVING-KINDNESS MEDITATION

Loving-kindness meditation is the usual English translation of a practice called metta bhavana. 'Metta' means 'love', in a non-romantic sense – friendliness or kindness. The practice comes from the Buddhist tradition and is essentially about cultivating love and warmth towards others – not just friends and family but those you feel neutral towards, find difficult or even dislike, and further outwards to all living beings.

A landmark study in 2008 at North Carolina University found that practising loving-kindness meditation for seven weeks increased participants' feelings of love, joy, gratitude, pride, interest, hope and awe and therefore general satisfaction with life. In terms specifically of relationships, practising this meditation has been shown to increase compassion, empathy and social connections.

In its most common form, the practice consists of five stages, each lasting for around five minutes. However, one study at Stanford University in 2008 found that even if practised in a short session of just ten minutes, the exercise increased feelings of social connection and positivity towards strangers.

✳ Find a comfortable place to sit, stand or lie. First concentrate on yourself and focus on feeling calm and peaceful. The practice is first directed towards oneself because the theory is that we cannot love others unless we love ourselves.

Let these feelings spread outwards, so you can feel love in your heart. You can say silently to yourself a phrase like 'May I be well. May I be happy. May I be safe.' Or you can imagine golden light flooding into your body. Adjust the words and images as you wish. Repeat the phrases or focus on the image of yourself flooded by golden light.

✳ Next, visualise a good friend, your partner or a family member and imagine them as clearly as you can. Concentrate on their good qualities and why you admire and love them. Let the feelings grow by repeating, 'May they be well. May they be happy. May they be safe.' Or imagine the golden light flooding into their body from yours. Sink into these feelings of warmth, love and friendliness. These two techniques can be used during the next three stages.

✳ Bring to mind someone you do not either like or dislike – be it a colleague, distant family member or someone that you do not really know but see around.

Reflect on their humanity and include them in your feelings of love and acceptance.

✳ Now think of someone you dislike. Try to avoid any strong negative feelings and instead imagine them positively and send your metta – or love – to them as well.

✳ In the last stage, think of all four people – yourself, your friend, the neutral person and the person you dislike – then visualise your feelings flowing outwards to everyone around you, from the town or area where you live, to your whole country and then to the whole world. Visualise waves of loving-kindness flowing outwards from your heart. Then let the images and feelings fade. Take some time to relax and breathe deeply and come back to the present.

WHO MAKES ME SMILE?

Who are the people in your life who make you feel happy, joyful and loved? Who do you go to when you need a dose of affection, advice or cheering on? From your childhood friends to favourite colleagues and other people who have come into your life and enriched it, list those special connections below:

....

....

....

....

....

....

....

....

....

....

....

....

....

....

....

Piglet: 'How do you spell "love"? Pooh: 'You don't spell it, you feel it.'

WINNIE THE POOH, A.A. MILNE

CREATE SOME LOVE DOODLES

Doodles can show your personality and reveal the state of mind you're in, because you're only half-conscious of what you're drawing while doodling. A little like dreams, doodles can reveal inner preoccupations too.

Draw some of your own love doodles. While you are doodling you might like to think about: The people you love and their unique attributes; what love means to you; symbols of love:

MY RELATIONSHIP BUCKET LIST

Ponder on those things that you have always wanted to do with your partner. It could be something as simple as getting a couple's massage, a tandem-bike ride or planning a trip to somewhere special; or maybe you've had more unusual ideas, like starting a new family tradition or making a time capsule of your life together and burying it in the back garden.

Make your bucket list below:

....

....

....

....

....

....

....

....

....

....

....

....

....

....

'The most beautiful things
in the world cannot be
seen or touched, they
are felt with the heart.'

THE LITTLE PRINCE, ANTOINE DE SAINT-EXUPÉRY

MAKE . . . A DATE NIGHT JAR

Everyone should have date nights, especially people who have kids and whose relationships have slipped down the priority list. Whether you have been together five months, five years or five decades, the date night is a ritual that should be faithfully observed: it allows for quality one-on-one time without any distractions.

More often than not we start out with good intentions to have a date night, mark it in our diaries . . . and then it completely falls by the wayside. This is where a Date Night Jar can come in handy.

Your date does not need to involve going out; it could just as easily be something you will do in an evening at home once the children are in bed. This craft idea is also a great way for thinking up some unusual date ideas.

Firstly, you will need a large jar – which you can decorate if you wish – some wooden lollipop sticks of four different colours and a marker pen. Decide on a category for each colour: I'd suggest Free, At Home, Going Out and More Expensive. Sit with your partner and think up some fun date ideas. Write them on the relevant stick. So for example if yellow is Free, red is At Home, blue is Going Out and green is More Expensive, ideas might include having a board games night (yellow), cooking an amazing three-course meal together (red), seeing an open-air cinema show (blue) or checking out an acclaimed new restaurant (green).

Mark a night out every week in your diary (both you and your partner need to do this!) and, as each weekly date comes round, decide which colour you want to go for and pick out a stick of that colour. No other planning needed!

A DEEP LISTENING EXERCISE

The average person speaks at 150 words a minute, but listens at 450 words a minute; this means we have spare brain capacity during conversation, so our minds tend to start to drift off and think about other things. Deep or mindful listening means listening to what another person has to say with your whole being. You let go of your thoughts, opinions, beliefs and reactions and just listen. Too often when we think, everything we hear comes with an automatic bias about how the words affect us. All too often we have jumped to conclusions before we have really heard what the other person has said. Being a good listener means being open-minded and genuinely interested in what the other person is saying, opening our awareness and letting go of reactive thinking.

Deep listening is made easier when our minds are calm and relaxed. If we are thinking about many things at once, we simply will not be able to tune in properly.

Try this exercise next time you are having an important conversation with a friend or family member:

❋ Stop anything else you have been doing. Take a few deep breaths.

❋ Look the other person in the eye and focus on them and what they are saying.

❋ Put aside all your worries and thoughts. If they pop into your head, do your best to ignore them and continue listening to the person talking to you.

❋ Listen to how the person is talking as well as their words – observe the tone of their voice, their posture and their gestures.

❋ Ask questions if you are unclear on something, but keep the queries open and do not change the subject.

❋ Let go of any judgement – recognise your opinions as just these – opinions, not judging – and continue to just listen.

How do I Love Thee,

ELIZABETH BARRETT BROWNING

How do I love thee? Let me count the ways.
I love thee to the depth and breadth and height
My soul can reach, when feeling out of sight
For the ends of Being and ideal Grace.
I love thee to the level of everyday's
Most quiet need, by sun and candle-light.
I love thee freely, as men strive for Right;
I love thee purely, as they turn from Praise.
I love thee with a passion put to use
In my old griefs, and with my childhood's faith.
I love thee with a love I seemed to lose
With my lost saints, I love thee with the breath,
Smiles, tears, of all my life! – and, if God choose,
I shall but love thee better after death.

MAKE . . . BREAKFAST IN BED
WHOLEMEAL BLUEBERRY PANCAKES

Surprising someone you love with breakfast in bed is always a lovely treat and if you can lounge for a while and eat breakfast with them, even better. These wholemeal pancakes are simple to make and taste delicious topped with maple syrup and extra fruit.

INGREDIENTS (FOR AROUND EIGHT PANCAKES):

120g wholewheat flour

100g plain flour

½ tsp cinnamon

1 tsp baking powder

300ml milk

1 tbsp honey or maple syrup

1 tsp vanilla extract

1 large egg

100g blueberries

Sunflower oil or butter for cooking

maple syrup (for topping – optional)

extra fruit (for topping – optional)

DIRECTIONS:

Mix the flours, cinnamon and baking powder together. In a separate bowl whisk the milk, honey or maple syrup, vanilla extract and egg until blended. Make a well in the centre of the flour and whisk the mixture in until combined, to make a smooth batter. Finally add the blueberries to the batter.

Heat a teaspoon of oil or knob of butter in the pan. Ladle in a small amount of batter and cook for three minutes over a medium heat, then flip and cook the other side until golden. Serve with maple syrup and extra fruit.

15 LOVE COUPONS I'D LIKE TO RECEIVE

When you have been married or together with someone for a long time, thinking of special treats for them can be hard. List the love coupons you would like to receive, they might be for specific date nights, back or foot rubs, or breakfast in bed:

....

....

....

....

....

....

....

....

....

....

....

....

....

....

....

THE BEAUTY OF A LOVE LETTER

Johnny Cash to his wife June Carter Cash on her 65th birthday in 1994

'Happy Birthday, Princess

We get old and get used to each other. We think alike. We read each other's minds. We know what the other wants without asking. Sometimes we irritate each other a little bit. Maybe sometimes we take each other for granted.

But once in awhile, like today, I meditate on it and realise how lucky I am to share my life with the greatest woman I ever met. You still fascinate and inspire me. You influence me for the better. You're the object of my desire, the #1 Earthly reason for my existence. I love you very much.'

Napoleon Bonaparte speaks of his love for Josephine de Beauharnais in 1796

'Since I left you, I have been constantly depressed. My happiness is to be near you. Incessantly I live over in my memory your caresses, your tears, your affectionate solicitude. The charms of the incomparable Josephine kindle continually a burning and a glowing flame in my heart ... I thought that I loved you months ago, but since my separation from you I feel that I love you a thousand fold more. Each day since I knew you, have I adored you more and more.'

Beethoven writes to his 'Immortal Beloved' in 1812

'Love demands everything and that very justly – thus it is to me with you, and you with me.'

CHAPTER 6

NURTURE

'Motherhood: All love
begins and ends there.'

ROBERT BROWNING

You're already running late for the nursery and school run and your toddler lies on the ground and kicks off their shoes in the middle of the pavement. Your other child is in a rush to see their schoolfriends and starts complaining about their sibling. Then they remind you it's gym day and where is their kit? Your phone starts ringing as you tell them they should remember it themselves and you can't be responsible for everything. You start to raise your voice and feel the people around you start to look as chaos ensues and you feel your heart start to hammer and tension settling in your face. Sound familiar?

Parenting is the hardest job we will ever do, and mindfulness experts extol the virtues of the practice when it comes to looking after babies, children and teenagers. If a child has a tantrum or starts shouting, it is because they are young and are still learning the ability to regulate their emotions. Parenting experts say that if we lose control in front of our children and proceed to shout back, this is terrifying for them and only exacerbates their feelings. Instead of the ideal of 'modelling' calm behaviour, we model aggressive reactions. At the same time our children are not learning to regulate their own emotions and self-soothe and if you ignore their need for comfort, the tantrum and their behaviour may get worse and carry on for longer. Parents who are able to weather their children's emotional ups and downs and manage their own reactions to their child's feelings are giving them a solid foundation for psychological well-being.

Our children are capable of setting off a huge range of emotions in us. By approaching them in a calm way, we give ourselves time to react, observe our negative feelings and then respond in a rational manner. We are then able to calm the storm of our children's anxieties by giving them a sense of safety. If we can do this, acknowledge their worries and then provide a calm solution, the situation will resolve itself far quicker and more harmoniously.

As well as helping us deal with stressful emotional situations ourselves, practising mindfulness around our children allows us to be more sensitive and attuned to their needs. When we are with them, rather than looking at our phones or tablets, we should really listen to them, showing them that we are there for them and that what they have to say is important to us. This doesn't mean agreeing to their every request or mollycoddling them but simply looking them in the eye, making physical contact and addressing their feelings.

Alongside this, if we help our children learn to become more mindful – something as simple and quick as some deep breathing every evening before bedtime – this will contribute to structural development in their brains and give them more emotional balance; they will be better equipped to deal with difficult situations in their lives around school, their peers and personal relationships.

Children can start to learn from a young age the ability to approach situations in a calmer way. Research has found that mindfulness training for children and young people increases attention, social awareness and other interpersonal skills. The cognitive processes known as executive functions also increase; this is a key factor in academic success as well as enhancing children's patience, compassion and happiness.

MY FAVOURITE MOTHERHOOD MEMORIES

From sniffing the newborn scent of your baby after bathtime, to building sandcastles with toddlers and those snatched moments in time where your heart simply fills as if it could explode with emotion, you no doubt have a catalogue of joyful motherhood memories.

List some of your favourites below:

....

....

....

....

....

....

....

....

....

....

....

....

....

....

....

THREE MINDFULNESS EXERCISES FOR MUM AND CHILD

Practising mindfulness with your children can be beneficial to you both. Sometimes as adults we do not realise that children experience stress too; they have their own personal pressures to do with parts of their lives including school, peers and exams. Children can also sense stress in their parents or the other people around them. They find it hard to recognise feelings of stress or be able to process them, so mindfulness exercises like these can help children become more aware of their own feelings and emotions.

FLOATING ON A CLOUD

Lie on your back and gently close your eyes. Imagine a fluffy cloud floating high in the sky above you and watch it slowly come down from the sky. What colour is it? Is it a bright white cloud that looks like a marshmallow? Or is it like a long, thin pillow? Climb on to your cloud and imagine floating away. Where does it take you? Go to a special place where you feel happy and peaceful. Describe what you see . . .

HUGGING MEDITATION

This exercise was developed by Buddhist monk Thich Nhat Hanh, who says that when we hug and connect our hearts, we know we are not separate beings. Mindfulness brings happiness and understanding to both parties.

Stand facing your child. Look into each other's eyes (if your child is small, kneel down so you can look them directly in the eye). Start to hug slowly and gently. Take three deep breaths. First focus on feeling present and alive, during the second breath focus on your child and in the third breath, feel grateful and happy that you are both alive and holding each other. Gently release your arms and look into your child's eyes. Place your palms together, show them how to do the same, and bow to each other to show thanks.

RAINBOW WALK

This is a simple exercise that you can do with your child regardless of their age and that can be done anywhere, at any time of year. It will quieten the mind and provide you both with some exercise.

The idea is to look for something in each colour of the rainbow; so you need to find something red, orange, yellow, green, blue, indigo and purple (violet). If your child is older they might like to take pictures of the colours with the camera on a phone, or they might want to write down what they have seen. Young children will want to discuss what they can see as you walk together. Enjoy focusing on the present moment and the scenes around you.

THINGS TO TEACH YOUR CHILD

* Shoot for the moon – even if you miss you'll land among the stars

* Never let go of the magic of Christmas

* Travel far and wide

* Always look on the bright side

* Rise to every challenge

* Treat others with kindness and respect

* Fight courageously, lose gracefully

* Keep your promises

* Believe in yourself

* Be curious

* Do what you love, love what you do

* Respect is at the root of all good things

* Welcome help and learn from everything

Add your own thoughts below ...

....

....

....

....

....

....

....

....

....

....

....

....

....

....

....

....

....

....

....

....

....

....

....

....

A LETTER . . . TO MY CHILD

How often do you tell your child what you love most about them and that you are proud of their unique talents, abilities and accomplishments? A letter is tangible and lasting, so no matter how old or young your child is, pick up a pen and write them a letter.

MAKE . . . A MIND JAR

Mind jars provide a healthy way for children (and adults) to calm down, take deep breaths and work through emotions. They are also lovely to look at and simple to make.

SUPPLIES:

Glass jar or plastic container
Hot water
Glitter glue
Superglue
Extra glitter (optional)
Food colouring (optional)

DIRECTIONS:

Take the jar and heat enough water to fill it almost to the top. It is best if the water is quite hot but not boiling, so the glue dissolves rather than clumping together. Take a measuring cup and add a lot of glitter glue in any colour. Stir it until it has dissolved. Add extra glitter and food colouring if you wish. Stick the lid down with superglue and shake it up. It will take about five minutes of shaking for the glitter to dissolve.

The glitter represents how busy the mind and body can be with thoughts and worries. Children can shake up the mind jar to show how they feel when they can't / would rather not say it verbally. Watching the glitter settle, and taking the chance to do some deep breathing while it does, helps our children and ourselves to self-regulate our emotions. Eventually the glitter will settle and the jar become clear and our minds will be more settled too. This reminds us that if we just take a short pause, we are in a position to respond to a situation skilfully, rather than impulsively.

A HAPPY FAMILY DOODLE

Draw your family in the car, on the sofa or in the house (and get your child or children to help if they wish). Be as creative as you wish and include all the extended family members who make you happy:

MAKE . . . SUPER SIMPLE POPPY SEED BREAD

Is there any smell nicer than that of freshly baked bread?
Bread is a such a fun food to make with kids and this super-
simple version can be made exactly as you and they like it,
with granary, wholemeal or white flour.

INGREDIENTS:

500g granary, wholemeal or white bread flour

7g sachet fast action dried yeast

½ tsp salt

25g poppy seeds

300ml warm water

2 tbsp olive oil

1½ tbsp clear honey

DIRECTIONS:

Mix the flour, yeast, salt and poppy seeds together in a large
bowl, then stir in the warm water, oil and honey to make a
soft dough. Knead the dough on a lightly floured surface until
it no longer feels sticky.

Oil the loaf tin and place the dough evenly in it. Pop the whole thing into a plastic food bag and leave to rise for an hour.

Heat the oven to 200C/(180 fan)/Gas 4. Cut the bread across the top so it can rise evenly and bake for 30–35 minutes until it is golden and risen. Tip onto a cooling rack and leave to cool.

To My Mother,

CHRISTINA ROSSETTI

To-day's your natal day,
Sweet flowers I bring;
Mother, accept, I pray,
My offering.

And may you happy live,
And long us bless;
Receiving as you give
Great happiness.

135

CHAPTER 7

JOURNEY

'Not all who
wander are lost.'

J.R.R. TOLKIEN

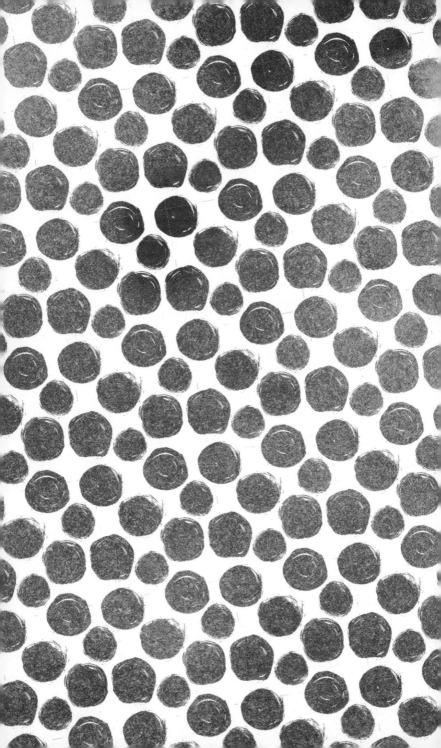

The significance of travel takes many forms, but most importantly it makes us happy. It is hard to describe that feeling of getting up early to catch a plane or standing on a railway station waiting to travel somewhere new. The mixture of excitement, expectation, fear and happiness is an ideal recipe for fun and adventure. Whether we travel for a short weekend away or a long holiday, in luxury or with just a backpack, travel makes us happier by increasing self-confidence, providing us with valuable new experiences and memories and breaking routine.

Travel often gives us some of the breathing space that we lose in our day-to-day lives. We can permit ourselves time to simply 'be', turn off our phones for a while and enjoy moments with the family and ourselves. Even a short trip can help us re-evaluate and appreciate our home and family life more.

However, holidays are for most of us a precious and fairly rare commodity; by being mindful, we can enjoy them to the best of our ability.

Travelling and holidays can also be very stressful. Whether it's packing for the whole family, organising everyone as they exit the house, or taking a wrong turn on the way to a destination, there are often issues and curveballs to deal with. Harnessing a mindful perspective means that you can acknowledge these annoyances while at the same time focusing on the present, so that the worries pass you by rather than hanging around. You can use mindfulness to take the time to be still and observe what you can see around you – it is the small details that will stay alive in your memory long after your time away is over. You will be better able to let go of any worries from home – be it about work, relationships or your sense of obligation as a mother – and be truly present.

I WAS HERE . . . CREATE A TRAVEL JOURNAL

Wherever in the world your travels and holidays take you, a journal makes a wonderful memoir and will also encourage you to be more mindful and look at all the new things around you. If your children are the right age and are travelling with you, they can also get involved and help – get them to include a photo and write about their favourite parts of the trip.

When writing your notes, think about the things you'll want to remember in ten, twenty or even thirty years' time. Use all your senses to describe what you see, smell, taste and hear and think of your journal as a personal memento, for you, rather than another thing you have to do. Keep it in your bag so that whenever something special happens, you can note it down immediately. Collect tickets, articles from local newspapers, menus, receipts and bottle labels, and anything else that takes your fancy and will make you think of your trip, and stick them in the journal. Or put them all in a clear plastic envelope at the back.

Consider everything that has made you smile that day. What did you learn? What did you see around you? What surprised you?

One of the best things about travel journals is that you can continue adding to them as you visit new places. The more pages you add, the more you can experiment with your creativity and inspire yourself to keep on travelling and seeing new places.

TIPS FOR MINDFUL COMMUTING

Of course not all our travels are about having holidays. The average British person commutes for fifty-four minutes a day. Often we find ourselves squashed into train carriages, shoulder to shoulder with other people, with our heads bowed, faces grey and all willing the time to go quicker. Or maybe you crawl to work in a car in back-to-back traffic jams. Our commutes can often leave us stressed and feeling negative.

Here are some ideas to practise to stay calm and mindful during the dreaded commute:

* Leave extra time if you can – knowing you're going to be late will just make you more stressed. If you arrive at your destination early, take the opportunity to have a coffee or enjoy the quiet at the office before your colleagues arrive.

* Stay mindful and notice the way your body feels. Are your shoulders and back straight? Where in your body can you feel tension? Consciously relax yourself and think about conserving energy for the rest of your day.

❋ Notice the details of the environment around you: the road, the train, the bus. What can you see, smell and hear?

❋ Take a few moments to focus on your breath. In a crowded train carriage, for example, this can create a welcome sense of space.

❋ Establish mindfulness rituals, so for example at each train or tube stop or, if you are driving by car, at each set of traffic lights, take a slow and deep breath.

PLACES I'D LIKE TO SEE: TELL A STORY

Where have you always dreamed of going? What do you think might be the world's most beautiful places? From ancient cities and epic waterfalls to underground worlds and awesome mountains, fill in your own story about where you would love to go, using these words to start you off:

Away	Wild
Freedom	Roam
Landscape	Trek
Sea	Live
Explore	Arrive
Boat	Drift
Train	Jaunt
Dream	Destination
Traverse	Fly
Journey	Lost
Discover	Escape

THE WONDER OF TRAVEL

'For mine is a generation that circles the globe and searches for something we haven't tried before. So never refuse an invitation, never resist the unfamiliar, never fail to be polite and never outstay the welcome. Just keep your mind open and suck in the experience. And if it hurts, you know what? It's probably worth it.'

THE BEACH, ALEX GARLAND

'At the end of hours of train-dreaming, we may feel we have been returned to ourselves – that is, brought back into contact with emotions and ideas of importance to us. It is not necessarily at home that we best encounter our true selves. The furniture insists that we cannot change because it does not; the domestic setting keeps us tethered to the person we are in ordinary life, but who may not be who we essentially are.'

THE ART OF TRAVEL, ALAIN DE BOTTON

'I can't think of anything that excites a greater sense of childlike wonder than to be in a country where you are ignorant of almost everything. Suddenly you are five years old again. You can't read anything, you have only the most rudimentary sense of how things work, you can't even reliably cross a street without endangering your life. Your whole existence becomes a series of interesting guesses.'

NEITHER HERE NOR THERE: TRAVELS
IN EUROPE, BILL BRYSON

THE CALM OF THE SEA

'The sea once it casts its
spell holds one in its
net of wonder for ever.'

JACQUES COSTEAU

Why do we head to the beach on holiday for a sense of
calm and togetherness? Since ancient times, water has
been thought to have healing and transformational
properties. In early Rome, baths were an important part of
cultural life and a place where people went to relax and
talk to each other in a tranquil environment. In Ayurveda,
a system of medicine with its roots in India, and in
traditional Chinese medicine, water is key to balancing the
body and mind.

A day by the sea can give us a sense of calm or clarity.
Whether we are swimming, sailing, scuba diving, surfing or
just lying by the ocean, being by the water provides us with
that sense of tranquillity. Blue, the shade of the sea, is a

much-loved colour and is traditionally associated with calmness, order, relaxation and loyalty.

Entrepreneurial scientist and marine biologist Wallace J. Nichols believes we all have a 'blue mind' and theorises that the mind enters a meditative state when we are in or near water. Brain scanning has shown that proximity to water makes the brain produce feel-good hormones like dopamine and oxytocin and also causes a drop in the stress hormone cortisol. Nichols believes that this is because the sight and sound of water is 'simple' and allows our brains a break, so we can be still.

SEARCHING FOR SHELLS

Stroll along the beach and make it your mission to find on the beach the most unusual items you can. Look closely at the different colours, textures and edges. Think about what you can do with the shells when you get home.

> 'To see the World in a Grain of Sand
> And a Heaven in a Wild Flower
> Hold Infinity in the Palm of your hand
> And Eternity in an hour.'

> FROM *AUGURIES OF INNOCENCE*,
> WILLIAM BLAKE

HAVE A DIGITAL DETOX

Nothing beats the simple pleasure of a holiday, when you are away from work and family pressures. That is until you reach for your phone to 'just quickly' check your email – and then, out of habit, find yourself on Twitter, Facebook or Instagram, all your usual news apps . . . and suddenly two hours have passed. With constant access to work and social media, our excessive reliance on technology is making us impatient, forgetful and distracted. The term 'digital detox' was added to the *Oxford English Dictionary* in 2013, just six years after the launch of the iPhone, and now half of all UK adults say they are 'completely hooked' on their smartphones.

Recently there has been huge growth in digital detox retreats, where we can completely unplug and be free of the reminders of modern life. From remote beach huts to mountain lodges, these holidays take us to places where our smartphones are completely useless.

Follow some or all of these tips for a complete digital detox:

❋ Let people know you will be offline for a few days

❋ Switch off your phone and hide it somewhere for the duration of your holiday

❋ Delete all the social media apps from your phone, so you're not tempted to check them

❋ Change your password so you can no longer get into your phone

❋ Welcome quiet time and enjoy being undisturbed by constant buzzing, texts and social media notifications

DIGITAL DETOX AT HOME:
UNPLUG FOR A DAY

While a holiday is the perfect excuse to take time away from the computer and other distracting technology, it is good to unplug at home too. It's unsurprising that we find it hard to disconnect even when we are on holiday; research suggests that 23 per cent of us come back from time away with what has been dubbed 'FOMO': fear of missing out by being offline. Therefore, it is also good to stop the cycle of bingeing on screen time and go offline more regularly. One study by technology company Kovert found that limited access to smartphones promotes better relationships and short-term memory, because we are more present and focused, as well as better sleep and an improved perspective on life in general.

To get started, keep track of how much time you spend online – on essential tasks, but also on non-essential browsing. Then plan what to do with your day offline and create a list of things you would like to do. It will allow you to break the online dependency, reclaim some time for you and your family, create space to do what really matters and cleanse your mind. Plan a digital detox – maybe monthly – and you'll be amazed at what you can accomplish in that time and how you feel afterwards.

Write down all the things you could do if you unplug for a day:

....

....

....

....

....

....

....

....

....

....

....

....

....

....

....

....

....

....

....

....

....

PEACEFUL WAVES
RELAXATION EXERCISE

Even if you are not near the sea, this exercise will help you to reap the same rewards as if you were by the ocean. You can do this for as little as sixty seconds or as long as thirty minutes . . .

❋ Sit or lie down. Close your eyes and imagine you are standing by the sea. Recall how you used to feel when you were on the beach as a child. Imagine the warmth of the sand between your toes and the gentle breeze against your body.

❋ Now visualise the beach. Think about the sand, the colour and texture of it. Imagine you are taking a few steps towards the sea. How does the sand feel between your toes? Look behind you and see your footprints.

❋ Listen to the rhythm of the waves rolling in and out. Consider the colour of the sea and way the colour changes at the edge of the sand. Listen to the sound of the waves rolling in and out. Look out at the

horizon and the sea glittering in the sunlight. Look at
where the surf meets the sky.

❋ Lie on the sand and allow yourself to become deeply
relaxed. Let comfort and warmth fill your body.

MY FAVOURITE HOLIDAY MOMENTS

Sticky-fingered ice cream hands, crabbing in rock pools, camping under the stars . . . some of our most joyful memories are the ones from times when we were away from home.

List your favourite holiday moments below:

....

....

....

....

....

....

....

....

....

....

....

....

....

....

....

MAKE . . . A TRAVEL MOODBOARD

Moodboards are a fun and creative device and can help you explore your ideas about travel. Think about the holidays and travels that you dream of: What do they look like? What are the common threads? Do they represent a feeling or emotion?

Collect images that represent these thoughts from newspapers, magazines and the Internet. Play around with them until you are happy with the images you have. You can use anything from four or five to around forty images. If you want to, use two or three key words to explain your vision, cut these out from magazines or write them and include them on the board.

Put your moodboard somewhere prominent in your house so you will look at it frequently and feel energised and inspired.

CHAPTER 8

WORK

'Choose a job you love
and you'll never have to
work a day in your life.'

CONFUCIUS

In the workplace, it seems that we are all being asked to do more with less, work longer hours and deal with increasingly heavy workloads. We work in a world of dizzying speed, fierce competition and exponential complexity. It is a culture where being busy, rushing from one task to another, working late and juggling a million and one tasks is seen as a badge of honour; but in fact this can be counterproductive.

Work is the area where many of us feel the most pressure. Stress now tops the league of reasons for long-term sickness absence and accounts for 38 per cent of working days lost per year.

Interest in applying mindfulness within the workplace is rising rapidly. Many individuals – and businesses – are realising that the benefits of mindfulness can be dramatic. As well as supporting overall well-being, mindfulness has been linked to improved cognitive function, enhanced creativity and communication and lower stress levels, all of which are obviously beneficial for employers. Mindfulness has now been introduced in workplaces such as Google, KMPG, GlaxoSmithKline, the Home Office, Transport for London, the NHS and PricewaterhouseCoopers.

A study at the University of Westminster revealed that practising mindfulness meditation builds self-confidence in leaders and inspires shared learning. And according to another report, the more mindful the manager, the lower the employee's emotional exhaustion and the higher their job satisfaction.

A study at the University of Washington showed that mindfulness affects the part of the brain responsible for self-regulation and that people who meditate can focus on tasks for longer and are less distracted by emails and web browsing.

There are many ways to start practising mindfulness and being calm at work and there are many books on the matter, but you can start simply – by taking a few one-minute breaks at your desk to just breathe. Take some time out every hour to inhale deeply and focus on your breath. If you feel yourself becoming stressed and anxious in a work situation, deliberately stop what you are doing and step away from your desk or the stressful environment, focus on your senses and breathing and try to relax your muscles.

HOW TO EMAIL MINDFULLY

Plagued by an in-box full of hundreds of unread emails? Pressed send then immediately wanted to retrieve the email? Many of us struggle to stay on top of our emails and fire them off at speed, without really considering the impact they can have. Email lacks the emotional signals and social cues of a face-to-face conversation, so it is easy to lose meaning and nuance and to offend people.

If you want to reduce the number of messages you receive, it might pay to examine your own email habits. According to a research team from the University of Glasgow and Modeuro Consulting, one the best ways to receive fewer emails is simply to send fewer. They asked the executives at a London based utilities company to think twice before sending an email and, as a result, email correspondence reduced by half.

Some tips for mindful emailing:

❉ Compose an email as you normally would.

❉ Stop and take a deep breath. If you are feeling strong emotions, take a minute out to focus solely on your breathing.

✳ Consider the recipient and result of the email: What do you want to achieve? Could you reword certain sections of your email to make your meaning clearer? Could anything in it be misunderstood?

✳ Look over your email again and make the appropriate changes.

✳ Do not send the email straight away but leave it in your drafts folder and do something else, then come back to it.

✳ Take one last look before you press the send button.

Ask yourself, did you need to send that email at all? When possible, always pick up the phone or walk over to a colleague to deliver the message.

FIVE YOGA STRETCHES YOU CAN DO AT YOUR DESK

Being seated at a desk all day can make you feel tired, irritable and achy. Just taking a few minutes, every few hours, to do some stretches at your desk can relieve stress, increase productivity and, most importantly, make you feel more calm:

SEATED BACKBEND

Sitting at your desk, take a deep breath, open your arms wide and then reach them up towards the ceiling. As you exhale. look upwards to your hands, which should be a little way behind you, and feel your upper chest expand. Hold for a few breaths and then release.

LEG CRADLE

Place your outer left ankle on your right thigh. Rest your right hand on your left ankle and your left hand on your left knee. Exhale and slowly bend forwards, while keeping your spine straight. Just go as far as is comfortable; you may feel a stretch in the outer thigh. Hold for thirty seconds and then repeat on the other side.

SEATED TWIST

Inhale deeply and, as you exhale, start to twist to your right. If your chair has an armrest, place both hands on it; if it is armless, rest your right hand on the chair behind you and your left hand on your right thigh. As you inhale, lengthen your spine and squeeze in your stomach. Use the exhalation to move further into the twist. Hold for thirty seconds and release, then repeat to the other side.

SHOULDER ROLLS

As you inhale, draw your shoulders up to your ears and back, then down and forward on the exhale, in a circular motion. Repeat three or four times and then reverse the movement.

WRIST AND FINGER STRETCHES

Constant typing builds up tension in your hands and fingers. Stand up and turn your hands so that your wrists are facing your computer.

Place the heels of your hands, and your fingers, flat on your desk. Lean into your wrists and flatten your palms as much as you can, feeling the stretch in the wrists and fingers.

MASTERMIND YOUR CAREER

Mind maps help you to visually and textually organise your ideas and thoughts. You can map where you would like your career to take you; or, if you are currently not working, you can use them to think about what you would like to do when or if you return to work.

Use a large notepad or sheet of paper. Start in the centre of the page and work outwards. Use colours and images – they encourage creative thinking – and think of it as an extended doodle that conveys meaning, with the main theme in the centre and ideas and thoughts emanating out. The brain works best like this and can express itself more freely. Connect all the branches together – the brain works by associating things with each other. Make your branches curved – research shows that they are more interesting for the brain.

Think about some or all of the following, depending on whether or not you're currently working:

❋ What you are doing now. Define your role and responsibilities.

✳ Add in your career goals, from short term (say six months to a year) to longer term (three to five years). What would you like to accomplish and what does the end result look like?

✳ Ask yourself why you love your work and what parts of your job you would like to do more of.

✳ What are your core values that you are not willing to compromise?

✳ What are your strengths and unique talents? What are you really good at right now and what would you like to be better at?

✳ Who are your role models and the people that you admire?

DON'T KNOW WHERE TO START?
TRY A PVT TRIANGLE

If you are a mum who has taken time out to start a family and wants to go down a completely different career path from the work you did before you had children, or you hate your job but don't know where to start when it comes to planning a new career, try this exercise. Draw a triangle with your **passions** at one point, your **values** at another and your **talents** at the third, hence the title 'PVT' triangle. Then try to pin down careers or jobs that integrate all three and list them in the middle.

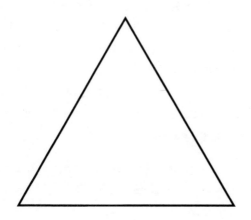

MAKE . . . RAW CHOCOLATE ENERGY BITES

When you've had a late night or broken night's sleep, chances are that at 3 p.m. you will be needing an extra boost of energy. Rather than reach for a chocolate bar, make some of these energy bites at the start of the week and keep them with you at work for an instant, guilt-free pick-me-up.

Cacao, or raw chocolate, is a guilt-free treat packed with benefits. It is chocolate in its purest form, made by simply cold-pressing cacao beans, and it contains many nutrients and minerals including magnesium, calcium, iron and potassium, along with fibre and protein. Cacao beans also contain natural chemicals called flavonoids, a type of antioxidant compound; they promote general health as well as having specific benefits including increasing the levels of neurotransmitters such as serotonin in our brains, making us feel more calm and happy.

These bites feel very rich and decadent and just one or two will keep those sugar cravings at bay. They can be kept in the fridge for up to a week.

INGREDIENTS (TO MAKE AROUND TWENTY BITES):

250g Medjool dates
125g shredded coconut
50g raw cacao powder
1 tsp vanilla extract
2 tbsp water
pinch of cinnamon
handful of pumpkin seeds
more shredded coconut for rolling

DIRECTIONS:

Put everything into a food processor and process until finely
mixed. You can add more water if the mixture needs it. Press
the dough into small balls and roll them in the coconut.
Freeze for one hour, then serve.

WINNING REASONS TO TAKE YOUR LUNCH BREAK

We are all looking for the perfect work/life balance, yet a survey by *BBC Breakfast* in 2013 found that 54 per cent of us are working through our lunch hours, while 53 per cent of us believe our colleagues do the same. Going by these figures, if everyone actually took their lunch break, we would all have an extra five hours a week or 240 hours a year.

The advantages of taking a lunch hour are huge. Most importantly, regular breaks help keep our brains and bodies healthy. One study at Humboldt University in Berlin found that if workers eat at their desks they are more stressed and less creative and productive. It is important to get outside, even just for a fifteen-minute walk – or even better, head to the gym. Researchers at Bristol University found that people who exercise are productive, happier and suffer less stress on the days when they go to the gym compared to the days that they don't. By exercising, either in a gym or outdoors, you will also have an opportunity to stretch your muscles and release pressure from your back; especially welcome if you are stuck behind a computer all day.

If you take a break, you will also be more productive in the afternoon. In the 1950s American physiologist Nathaniel Kleitman discovered that we sleep in roughly ninety-minute cycles, moving from light to deep sleep and back again. A decade later, he discovered that our waking hours also follow this cycle; we lose focus every ninety minutes and, without a break of approximately twenty minutes, get drowsy or hungry. We tend to counteract these feelings by consuming more coffee or sugar and forcing our bodies to keep going, when the natural thing to do would be to take some time away from our desks.

If you leave your desk during the working day, you'll eat more mindfully and be better able to resist hitting the vending machine. It is also an opportunity to eat lunch with your colleagues occasionally, which is important as healthy connections with your colleagues improve overall job satisfaction; one study in 2008 at the Massachusetts Institute of Technology found that workplace socialising during breaks significantly improves productivity.

Here are some ideas for activities for your lunch break:

- ✳ Work out at the local gym or take a brisk walk
- ✳ See a show or take in a free lunchtime concert

✳ Visit a local gallery or museum

✳ Browse a local market

✳ Volunteer in a local soup kitchen or animal shelter

✳ Learn a new skill, like taking a cooking class or online language course

✳ Start a book club or knitting club for your colleagues

✳ Plan a holiday

✳ Read a book

✳ Have a manicure or massage

Add your own ideas below:

....

....

....

....

....

....

....

....

....

....

....

....

WAYS TO MAKE
YOUR DESK AWESOME

Office space is often not particularly exciting or inspiring. It has been proven that your environment can seriously affect your productivity and energy levels, so white walls, a blank desk and fluorescent lighting might not be the most stimulating space. However, there are ways you can create a personal and striking desk space for yourself.

Here are some ideas:

* To start with, your space will look much better if it is clean, organised and tidy

* Raise your computer to eye level with a stack of your favourite hardback books, records or magazines so you are not straining your neck

* Get a plant or bring in bunches of flowers to add some life and colour

* Add a lamp with a soft light to create instant atmosphere

❋ Put some artwork into matching frames to create your own personal gallery

❋ Treat yourself to some original, bright and colourful office supplies – think neon staplers and bright notebooks

❋ Buy a mug that makes you smile or feel inspired

❋ Use a pretty and bright tray organiser

❋ Make your chair more comfortable by using a textured cushion

❋ Get a tiny personal fridge for under your desk

❋ Have pictures around you that make you smile – photographs of family and friends, or postcards you have collected during your travels

❋ Keep little trinkets that people have given you in a small dish

❋ Pin up inspirational quotes

❋ Put a multicoloured rug on your floor

'Your work is going to fill
a large part of your life,
and the only way to be
truly satisfied is to do what
you believe is great work.
And the only way to do
great work is to love what
you do. If you haven't
found it yet, keep looking.
Don't settle. As with all
matters of the heart, you'll
know when you find it.'

STEVE JOBS

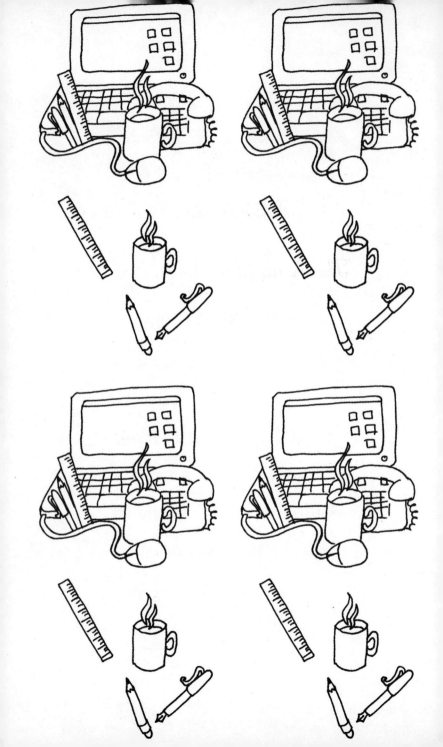

CHAPTER 9

SPACE

'There's no place like home.'

THE WIZARD OF OZ

In an ideal world, our homes would be an oasis of calm. They are our sanctuaries: where we sleep, rest, eat, laugh, play and take refuge from the stresses and demands of the world – yet all too often, even at home, it feels hard to find calm. There is always too much to be done and no time to do it.

More and more of us are working from home; an ONS report from 2014 showed that over 4 million people – or 13.9 per cent of the working population – now work remotely. Unless you are lucky enough to have a separate workspace, it can be hard to keep working life and home life separate. As someone who works from the dining table, I find it almost impossible to switch off and am often still responding to emails late at night. We are also more connected to the wider world than ever before, via our computers, smartphones, iPads and laptops, so there often seems to be no reason – or chance – to stop working or communicating with the outside world.

Our homes need to be somewhere we can retreat to, where we can restore calm and truly live in the moment. Whether it is keeping your home as ordered as possible, using soothing colours on the walls, or playing music and having calming scents, every small touch helps. As well as separating work and home lives, it is also worth factoring in regular downtime free from excessive stimulation, and allowing yourself time to 'do nothing', so you can rest and do exactly what you want, whether it's daydreaming, reading a book or lying back in a luxurious, scented bath.

SIMPLE TRICKS TO DETOX YOUR HOME AND BODY

Feeling tired, drained or out of synch? Whether you are trying to get back on track with your diet and health, or simply looking to create good habits, there are many ways to detox your way to feeling better. Detoxing has been practised by cultures around the world for centuries – Ayurvedic and Chinese medicine systems both make use of it – to rest, cleanse and nourish the body. Detoxification is said to protect us from disease and renew our ability to maintain optimum health.

The best way to flush out toxins from our bodies is by drinking lots of water and eating a diet packed full of nutrients and less processed foods; but toxins find their way into our bodies through more than just food. We are exposed to many chemicals in our homes. Here are some easy ideas to help minimise chemicals and toxins:

Use Epsom bath salts: Hot water draws toxins out of the body to the skin's surface and cool water pulls them away from the skin. Epsom bath salts make the body sweat and speed up the detoxification process.

Add lemon juice to your drinking water: Lemon cleanses and alkalises the body and gives a welcome injection of Vitamin C, which boosts the immune system.

Have a shoe-free household: Make everyone take their shoes off at the door; most dirt and pesticides come into the home via shoes. Go barefoot indoors, or have a selection of slippers for family and guests by the door.

Give yourself a body brush: Dry body brushing is an easy and effective way of helping to detox your body. It will improve the appearance of your skin by eliminating dead skin cells and stimulating blood circulation.

Open your windows and doors regularly: Indoor air is full of dust, debris and bacteria that without proper ventilation will circulate and build up. Even when it is cold, open the window and let some fresh air in for just five minutes.

Swap your cleaning products for greener ones: Ditch the harsh versions for more green brands or use natural ones, such as vinegar in the place of bleach or baking soda to scrub tiles.

Think seasonal and organic: Stick to foods that are as close to nature as possible. The fewer ingredients in a product the better; and if you do not understand an ingredients list – don't buy the food.

Work out: One of the best ways to eliminate toxins from the body is to exercise. Aside from losing those extra pounds and sweating out toxins, exercising is associated with a host of other benefits and aids bodily systems including circulation, respiration and digestion.

Cut back on alcohol: The liver filters alcohol but also has 500 other functions and if it's busy filtering out the alcohol it's going to need to work harder to fulfil it's other functions. Drinking too much also taxes your central nervous system and kidneys and may impair your body's ability to cleanse itself naturally.

Fill your house with plants: They help to keep the air clean and rid your home of harmful toxins.

Get a water filter: While our tap water in the UK is considered safe to drink, it still contains chemicals your body would be better off without, so buy a water filter and keep it topped up and in the fridge.

MAKE . . . SOME FRESH CLEANSING JUICES

Fresh juices have the power to cleanse and nourish and juicing is a great way of incorporating more fresh fruit and vegetables into your diet. They provide us with minerals, vitamins, essential fatty acids, proteins and much more and can be made quickly and easily a couple of times a week to supplement your diet.

Here are some simple and delicious ideas. Each recipe makes one to two glasses, depending on how large a glass you like.

ULTIMATE GREEN JUICE

This juice is loaded with potassium, folic acid, calcium, iron and essential amino acids and antioxidants, which are important for cleansing and fighting free radicals.

1 celery stick

¼ cucumber

1 green apple

1 small bunch of parsley

1 small handful of spinach

1 lime

BEETROOT ENERGY JUICE

Beetroot is a powerful cleanser of the blood and highly nutritious. It has also been shown to increase stamina, boost brain power and lower blood pressure. Add apple for extra sweetness and always put your ginger between chunks of apple or carrot, so it gets pushed through the juicer properly.

1 beetroot
1 apple
½ inch of fresh ginger
1 carrot
½ lemon
1 cup coconut milk

FRESH START MELON JUICE

Melons are great for juicing because of their high water content; they are also packed with essential vitamins and minerals. Broccoli is also rich in Vitamins A, C, E and K. This is a great juice to start the day and is also very family-friendly.

¼ peeled galia or cantaloupe melon
some broccoli florets
¼ medium-sized sweet potato
dash of cinnamon

'Have nothing in your house that you do not know to be useful, or believe to be beautiful.'

WILLIAM MORRIS

CREATE SPACE BY
CLEARING CLUTTER

Do you often feel overwhelmed by the amount of stuff you own? Do you find yourself constantly tripping over things or never able to find what you are looking for? How many times have you promised yourself you are going to 'get organised' but it hasn't happened? The best way to create a calm environment is to try to limit clutter. This is easier said than done when you have children at home, of course, but it is hard to feel calm when you are constantly hunting for a clean pair of socks, have misplaced your child's favourite teddy or your dry cleaning ticket is lost for ever. When we look for things, we waste time and emotional energy feeling frustrated. Time is the currency we can not get back.

How do you feel when you look at clutter? Stressed, anxious or annoyed? Researchers at Princetown University Neuroscience Institute in the US found that physical clutter affects our ability to focus and process information. This wears down our mental resources so we're more likely to become frustrated.

Here are some tips to get you started:

✳ Empty the bins regularly and recycle everything you can, including all old newspapers and magazines.

✳ Designate a spot for incoming post and papers. Designate an in-box tray or place in your home where all letters, school newsletters, bills, receipts and manuals go.

✳ If you have young children at home, aim for one no-clutter zone – this could be an entire room or a space within one. Insist that everything is put away so this one zone stays clear.

✳ Identify what is important – which toys are truly important to your children? What do they play with and love? Get rid of the things you no longer want – give them to friends or charity shops, or recycle. Try to aim for a 'one in one out' rule with new items.

✳ Always make your bed and straighten the sheets, pillows and duvet – it will instantly make the room look better.

✳ Try to buy less. From bottles of shower gel that just clutter up the bathroom to kids' toys, rather than spending money on lots of things, try to buy quality items instead.

✳ Create easy storage systems, so coats go on hooks, there are labelled boxes and bins for toys and somewhere to hang the keys.

✳ Clean as you go and never leave a room empty-handed – take dirty cups or clothes that need washing with you.

✳ At the end of the day before you turn in, spend five minutes tidying the kitchen or straightening up the sitting room. It will help you start the following day in a calm way.

✳ Allow mess. If you have young children it is impossible for there never to be mess. Let them play and make a mess, but always insist they tidy up afterwards or, if they are young, that they help you put their toys away.

✳ Store kitchen appliances out of sight. If you have a food processor or a juicer on your work surfaces, or other appliances that you do not use on a daily basis, keep them in a cupboard instead.

WHAT I LOVE ABOUT WHERE I LIVE

When we make the same journey over and over again – to and from our home, the familiar paths around the streets where we live, we can lose the ability to see what is special about our homes, neighbourhoods and communities. Write down why you love the place you live:

....
....
....
....
....
....
....
....
....
....
....
....
....
....
....
....
....

THE SECRETS OF SCENT

Have you ever stopped just a moment longer outside a bakery to savour the smell of freshly baked pastries, or paused to breathe in the heady scent of roses in a garden? Our sense of smell is directly linked to memory and the emotional centre of the brain. By using scent in our homes – be this candles, oil diffusers, room sprays or similar – we can improve our mood and create a serene environment. Our associations with certain smells differ, so if you find a particular smell soothing, use it and it will become associated with feeling calm.

Chamomile: Renowned for encouraging peace and calm. It soothes muscles and is often used as a sleep remedy. A recent study at University of Nottingham Medical School found that chamomile significantly relaxed blood vessels and smoothed muscle fibres.

Neroli: This delicate scent, derived from the blossom of the orange tree, calms, and soothes.

Jasmine: This scent is said to produce feelings of optimism and helps relieve nervous exhaustion, depression and stress-related conditions. Jasmine increases GABA activity (a chemical within the brain that improves mood) which helps regulate feelings of stress, anxiety and overexcitement. Researchers at Ruhr University in Germany have found that the brain can respond as well to jasmine as to sedatives and barbiturates; and tests have showed that jasmine dramatically calmed mice when their cage was filled with it.

Lavender: This has potent relaxation properties and has been shown to improve sleep and soothe tired muscles.

Rosemary: This is a stimulating and uplifting scent and very good for relaxing muscles. Studies show that smelling Rosemary produces beta waves, which improves alertness. A University of Nottingham study in around 2005 found a link between smelling rosemary and scoring higher on mental tests.

Frankincense: With its comforting, warm and exotic aroma, frankincense is said to slow breathing and has been shown to have a calming effect on emotions.

Rose: This fragrance is associated with female well-being, and is said to particularly help women who are suffering from depression, tension or relationship worries.

Sandalwood: Thought to have relaxing and calming qualities, this is used as an aid in yoga and meditation. In

India sandalwood oil is regarded as sacred. It works well to balance both the emotions and the immune system.

Geranium: Geranium has a restorative and calming effect and helps to balance stress hormones produced by the adrenal glands, giving a soothing effect on the whole nervous system.

Vanilla: The scent of pure vanilla makes us feel calm and at home; some aromatherapists say this is because it is the closest scent to a mother's milk. It has the ability to soothe and stimulate mental clarity.

Marjoram: This was known as the 'herb of happiness' to the ancient Romans and labelled 'joy of the mountains' by the Greeks. A muscle relaxant and anti-inflammatory, it has sleep-promoting properties.

Orange: A study at Mie University in Japan found that patients suffering from depression who had orange fragrance administered to them were able to markedly reduce the quantity of antidepressants they took. In 2000, researchers at the University of Vienna's Neurological Clinic examined the response to orange scent in a dentist's waiting room. The scent had a relaxing effect, notably on women. Compared to patients not exposed to the scent they had lower anxiety, felt more positive and were calmer.

'Scent is the most intense
form of memory'

JEAN-PAUL GUERLAIN

COLOUR ME CALM

There is something very special about a bed made up with pure white linen or a blue living area; they seem to exude Zen-like calm. We all associate colour with mood, but colour therapy takes this idea one step further and believes that colour has the power to improve our sense of well-being.

The idea of colour therapy is not a new one. The ancient Egyptians, Greeks and Chinese all had had 'colour halls' or rooms painted different colours, which were used for treating and healing ailments.

Colour is simply light in varying wavelengths and, as such, is a form of energy. Colour therapists believe that the different vibrational energy of each colour has an effect on how we feel:

Violet: Calming for the mind and body and is thought to be purifying.

Blue: Tones of blue are generally relaxing and calming and promote serenity and the release of tension.

Green: Balancing and harmonising, and encourages tolerance. Olive green symbolises peace.

Indigo: This is thought of as a spiritual colour, and is associated with healing and opening up the intuition.

Yellow: Specifically, a light lemon shade – stimulates mental activity and promotes feelings of confidence.

Orange: A gentle orange colour is warming and energising and can lift mood and banish depression and boredom.

Pink: Red is generally thought too stimulating a colour for the home but light pinks and rose are soothing and nurturing tones.

White: White contains all the colours and is said to be cleansing and purifying and to calm the heart, mind and emotions.

HAVE A LONG SOAK IN THE BATH

Baths might be more beneficial than you think. They are not only good for unwinding and soaking away the stresses of the day, which most of us know already; they can also improve cardiovascular health, boost the immune system and ease tension headaches. So the next time you feel stressed, turn on the taps and climb in . . .

* Use a scented oil to help you feel more relaxed. Pour it in when the bath is half full, and not directly under the taps, so it disperses evenly.

* The best temperature to relax the body is between 90 and 95 degrees Fahrenheit (32–35 in Celsius). This will open pores and encourage the body to sweat and release toxins.

* Use a body scrub to buff away dead skin cells and enhance circulation.

* If you have a headache, a cooled eye mask or cucumber slices over your eyes will help.

✳ Ensure your bathroom is warm and you have a fluffy bathrobe and slippers waiting for when you get out of the bath, to continue the feeling of cosiness and calm.

✳ Play relaxing music if you wish, or use a recorded guided meditation to induce a tranquil state.

✳ Dot candles around the bath to help create a blissful atmosphere.

✳ Don't be tempted to get out too soon; and switch off your phone so you are not disturbed. Relax for at least an hour afterwards to continue the feeling of calm.

DON'T UNDERESTIMATE THE POWER OF MUSIC

Music has the unique ability to tap straight into our emotions and make us feel calm and relaxed, or energised and alert. Whether we are moved by the power of Mahler's Fifth Symphony, or find ourselves singing along to Pharrell Williams's 'Happy', music is extremely powerful for enhancing well-being and as a unique tool to combat stress. Music also distracts us and absorbs our attention, making it a great aid to meditation and practising mindfulness.

Music is said to be most calming when the rhythm is slower than our heartbeat. This speed of music is thought to have beneficial effects on our physiological functions and to slow our heart rate, lower blood pressure and decrease the levels of stress hormones in the body. Slow and calming music resonates with the alpha wave pattern in our brains, associated with relaxation and deep calm. In one study, students performed an oral presentation with either Pachelbel's Canon in D or no music in the background. Those people who listened to the classical music had lower heart rates, reduced blood pressure and stress levels.

Certain music is said to induce sleep and one 2006 study at Stanford University discovered that music is able to change brain functioning to the same extent as medication.

Music can benefit our psychological well-being, too. Research from the University of Missouri published in the *Journal of Positive Psychology* definitively proved music can increase our happiness. It has also been shown that listening to music can help reduce stress and anxiety in hospital patients both before and after surgery, and can reduce burnout in students.

So whether it is listening to music while you work out, joining a choir or having the radio on while you work, just a few minutes' music each day can make you feel uplifted and energised.

MY HAPPY PLAYLIST

What music makes you feel uplifted, happy and evokes some
of your best memories? List your favourite, most powerful
songs or pieces below:

....
....
....
....
....
....
....
....
....
....
....
....
....
....
....
....
....
....
....

DRAW A CALM HOUSE

Here is a child's-style house with four rooms, a front door and some windows. Who or what would be in each room? Why would they be there? What makes you feel calm about your house? Draw people, words and images to represent the people and objects that would be in each room.

TAKE SOME TIME OUT TO READ . . .

When the nights draw in, the kids are in bed and the temptation is to switch on the TV to stare blindly at it for a few hours before going to bed, why not pick up a book and read instead? Reading can transport us to all kinds of places, boost our mood and induce calm.

Aside from the obvious benefits of gaining knowledge and mental stimulation, reading every day has been shown to improve memory and reduce stress. A 2009 study at the University of Sussex revealed that reading for as little as six minutes a day reduced stress levels by up to 68 per cent, while research from the University of Liverpool has found that readers are 21 per cent less likely to report feelings of depression and 10 per cent more likely to report good self-esteem than non-readers.

Make time for reading and create your own ritual. Here are the ingredients for the perfect reading session:

❋ Shed the denim jeans and stiff clothing and put on your most comfortable, soft clothing instead.

❋ Whether you lie on your bed or on a sofa or sit on a chair, make sure you have a soft blanket or throw to cover you and enough cushions to get cosy. Mix different textures for ultimate comfort.

❋ You don't want the lights to be too overwhelming, but you must be able to see the pages without straining your eyes. Try a desk lamp or table lamp behind one of your shoulders for soft, yet clear, lighting.

❋ Make a cup of tea to accompany your reading session. If you like herbal teas, a relaxing chamomile or green tea infusion is ideal, while simple Earl Grey is great for traditionalists.

'East or West, home is best'

DUTCH PROVERB

CHAPTER 10

CREATE

'Creativity is a gift. It doesn't come through if the air is cluttered.'

JOHN LENNON

You may work outside the home or not: whatever you do, whether you feel that your job is creative or that it could be more so, or if you just feel that you'd like more creativity in your life, kick-starting your creativity can enrich your life and help you discover what inspires you. Creativity is not just about drawing pictures; it is about finding different solutions to problems in everyday life. Creativity is not a rare gift that just a few of us are born with, but an integral part of everyone's make-up, albeit one that expresses itself differently in different people.

Mindfulness is said to boost our creativity. In 2012, a study at the University of Groningen and North Dakota State University looked at whether mindfulness affects awareness and the filtering out of other mental processes during creative tasks. They found that mindfulness improved 'insight' problem-solving, which is seeing and solving problems in different ways. Another study at Leiden University in the

Netherlands found that mindfulness improved problem-solving and divergent thinking – a style of mental processing that allows you to generate more ideas.

When you practise mindfulness you are stepping back from your emotions and thoughts, so that you can approach and solve whatever problem you are tackling more effectively.

THE POWER OF PLAY

As children we are all playful and creative. Our young minds are open to new experiences, possibilities and ways of doing things. As we get older we form 'ruts' in our way of thinking and we accept that things need to be done in a certain way. We also self-censor and worry about what others think, stopping us from being creative and playful.

Play in itself is seen as not something adults should do – as we get older we tend to think we should get serious. The only playing we do might be the odd game of competitive sport or board games. However, while we instinctively know that children should be allowed to play to help their brains develop and for them to relax and understand how the world works, we grow up and somewhere along the line we lose the ability to allow ourselves to play. Play is seen as unproductive and useless and – particularly as women – all too often we feel guilty about taking time out in this way.

Research shows that playing as adults is important: it makes us happy, and helps us with problem-solving and in our relationships. In his book *Play*, US psychiatrist and founder of the National Institute for Play, Stuart Brown, argues that playing is about more than just having fun and helps us build complex, responsive and socially adept brains. Defining what play is, he says it is 'a state of being' and is 'purposeless, fun and pleasurable'. For the most part the fun is in the experience, not the end goal.

Brown has spent decades taking 'play histories' from patients after realising when working with a group of homicidal young men that it was absent from their childhoods. He discovered that those who do not play are often joyless and depressed. He argues that play of any type – he has seven categories in total – is essential to brain development. 'Nothing lights up our brains like play,' he says.

Play can relieve stress, improve brain function, stimulate the mind and boost creativity, keep you energised and improve relationships and connections to others. It comes as no surprise that in Denmark – regularly noted as the happiest country in the world – the citizens benefit from flexible working conditions and affordable childcare, leading to more free time for sport and other 'play'-based fun. There is also more gender equality – parents share more of the household and parenting duties, giving mothers the opportunity to pursue their own interests. Academics contend that women in the UK, by contrast, feel they have to earn this kind of time out by getting to the end of their to-do list, which of course never comes.

Forward-thinking organisations like Google, Virgin and Pixar have also harnessed the power of play at work, understanding that it can boost productivity and therefore profits. We should all play, even if it is just for five minutes a day. So next time you go to the park, see the monkey bars and fancy a swing? You know what to do.

19 IDEAS FOR PLAY

Embrace your inner child and relearn the joy of giving yourself time to play. If you have children at home who can join in – even better! Here are some ideas:

1. Jump in puddles

2. Hula hoop

3. Have a pillow fight

4. Learn a magic trick

5. Fly a kite

6. Head to a dance class

7. Hit a piñata

8. Play sardines

9. Play Truth or Dare

10. Have a go at silent charades

11. Climb trees

12. Have a food fight

13. Put on a puppet show

14. Sing in the shower

15. Do some face painting

16. Have a water fight

17. Build a blanket fort

18. Make friendship bracelets

Now add your own ideas below:

....

....

....

....

....

....

....

....

....

....

....

....

....

....

....

....

....

....

....

....

....

....

....

....

TELL A STORY:
A CREATIVE MINDFULNESS EXERCISE

Take a photograph; it can be an old picture of yourself or someone else. Take a piece of paper and pen and sit down in a quiet place. Set a timer for ten or fifteen minutes and just start writing. Do not censor yourself and include as many emotions as possible. Enjoy focusing on the moment.

30 CIRCLES

Developed by US creativity researcher Bob McKim and popularised by designer Tim Brown, the 30 circles challenge is said to boost creativity. Take a pen and set a timer for three minutes. In this time, 'fill' as many circles as you can, focusing on quality not quantity. A drawing can incorporate more than one circle and you can draw animals, shapes, doodles, words, objects . . .

As well as alone, try doing this as an exercise with your children and compare results.

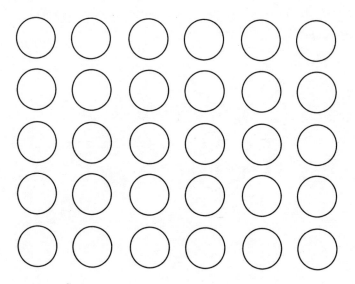

THE USELESS OBJECTS EXERCISE

Think of ten objects around your house. Write them down on a piece of paper. For each object think of as many uses as you can – don't worry if they sound silly.

When you look at these objects in the future, you will see them in a whole new light. For example, a pencil might not just be an object to write with but could turn into a back scratcher, houseplant stake, string holder, chopstick, doorstop, dog stick, pointer, ruler, bookmark, cuticle stick, drink stirrer . . .

'Every child is an artist;
the problem is staying an
artist when you grow up.'

PABLO PICASSO

THINGS I'D LIKE TO MAKE
WITH MY OWN TWO HANDS

What have you always dreamed of making? Fancy knitting a
scarf, sewing an item of clothing for your child, or having a go
at upholstering an old chair? List your creative ideas below:

....

....

....

....

....

....

....

....

....

....

....

....

....

....

....

....

....

....

30-DAY PHOTOGRAPHY CHALLENGE

Most of us have phones with cameras, so this exercise should be quite easy. All you need to do is to take the best picture you can every day for thirty days, based around the topics below. Start whenever you like and experiment as much as you can, with colours, composition and filtering.

1. Self-portrait
2. Love
3. Food
4. Home
5. Symmetry
6. A skyline
7. Flowers
8. Black and white
9. Shadows
10. Sleep
11. Water
12. Clouds
13. Hands
14. Animal
15. Someone you love
16. Something you love
17. Something blue
18. Something pink
19. Routine
20. Dark
21. In my bag
22. The best part of my day
23. Heart
24. Upside down
25. Bathtime
26. Insect
27. Sign
28. Cup
29. Mirror
30. Calm

'You can't use up creativity.
The more you have,
the more you have.'

MAYA ANGELOU

COLOURING – IT'S NOT JUST FOR CHILDREN . . .

Do you have vivid memories of taking your precious coloured pencils and colouring for hours at a time when you were younger? Perhaps your own children do a lot of colouring now?

The simple act of colouring has become increasingly popular among adults over the last couple of years and is now an international trend. Why the success? Experts say that it is because colouring is such an easy way to both calm the mind and occupy our hands.

Simple tasks that require repetitive motion create a state of peace because they force the mind to focus on the moment and not dwell on intrusive thoughts. This type of relaxation lowers the activity of the amygdala, the part of our brain affected by stress. Colouring also requires just the right amount of exertion, so that we can relax without feeling bored. Psychologists refer as this concept – the fine line between anxiety and boredom – as 'flow'.

Some experts also say that colouring also brings out our imaginative side and transports us back to our childhoods, a time when life was a lot less stressful. We can decide which colours we like and which pencils to choose and then watch as the picture comes to life. Psychologists also believe that creating something, whatever it is, can improve our moods and that the discipline of colouring means the activity blends creativity and comfort.

So go ahead, unleash your inner artist. Stick to the lines, or colour outside of them . . . you can do whatever you choose.

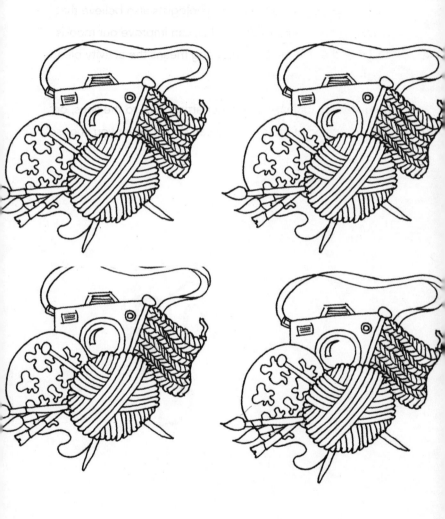

CHAPTER 11

FUTURE

'They say if you dream
a thing more than once,
it's sure to come true.'

SLEEPING BEAUTY

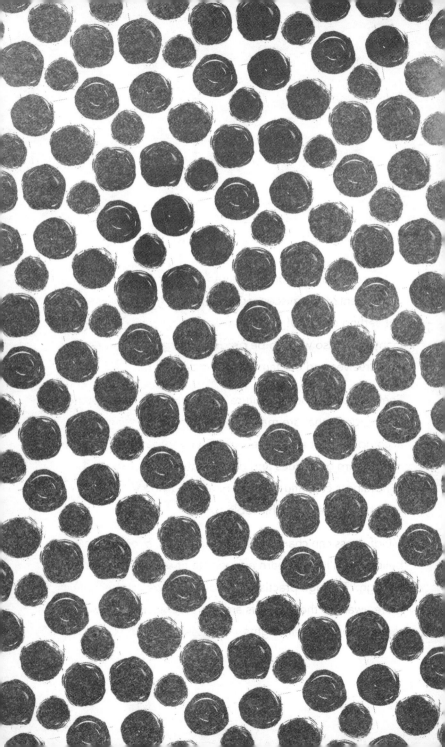

How do you plan for the future while still living in the present? It's a misconception that living mindfully means not setting goals. Of course we want to be peaceful, but many of us also want to be productive and build better lives for ourselves and our families at the same time.

Feeling good about the future is important for our happiness. Having goals that are manageable brings a sense of accomplishment and achievement. Goals are a way in which we can turn our values and dreams into a reality. And mindfulness can influence our goals by giving them a more realistic, gentle and achievable tone.

Mindfulness can change our limiting beliefs about ourselves, beliefs like 'I'll never earn enough/be fit enough/be confident enough.' Through practising mindfulness, we can become more aware of these beliefs and start replacing them with more encouraging thoughts.

The skills that are used in mindfulness help us to better screen out the negative thoughts that can undermine our health and well-being. It also gives us more attentional control and mental flexibility. Cultivating mindfulness helps us achieve our goals because we become able to focus on one task at a time, more self-aware and become able to understand ourselves with better clarity.

THE FUTURE-
SELF FILM MEDITATION

This exercise will help inspire you to make changes in your personal or working life. The more often you practise this, the more able you will become to create new thought and behaviour patterns.

❋ Sit or lie back somewhere you will not be disturbed and close your eyes. Focus on your breath. Imagine you are walking down ten steps and breathe slowly as you count down each step.

❋ As you get to the final step, imagine seeing a screen in front of you. Create in your mind a scene in which you see yourself in the future, be it with your husband, children or in the job of your dreams.

❋ See yourself on the screen and visualise the scene clearly. You are happy and contented. Who is there? What conversations are you having? Observe the world around you – are you outside with birds singing and leaves swaying in the breeze? Feel the mood and joy of the situation around you.

 Continue to imagine the scene for as long as you like before slowly opening your eyes and taking a few deep breaths to return to the here and now.

LIVES I'D WANT TO LEAD IF I HAD NINE LIVES

If you had more than one life, whose life would you like and why?

....
....
....
....
....
....
....
....
....
....
....
....
....
....
....
....
....
....

HAPPINESS IS . . .

- Blowing bubbles

- The sound of popcorn popping

- The chocolate bar at the back of the cupboard you forgot you had

- Spooning

- Hotel breakfasts

- Simplicity

- Old schoolfriends

- Flipping pancakes

- Building a treehouse

- An unexpected bouquet

- An airport reunion

- Freshly washed hair

- Sharing an umbrella

- The smell of rain on the pavement

✳ Sleeping in fresh sheets

✳ A cold shower on a hot day

✳ Your favourite song coming on the radio

✳ Waking up to sunshine on your face

✳ Making a new friend

✳ Peeling an orange in one peel

✳ New shoes that fit perfectly

✳ Children making each other laugh

Add your own thoughts below:

....
....
....
....
....
....
....
....
....
....
....

THE LISTS I'D LIKE TO MAKE ONE DAY

Whether you are new to list-making, list averse or love the creative process of filing thoughts and actions, list-making can be cathartic. Write down the lists you intend to make one day:

....

....

....

....

....

....

....

....

....

....

....

....

....

....

....

....

....

THE FUTURE TREE

Fill in this tree with the ideas and hopes you have for the future:

239

'The future depends on
what you do today.'

MAHATMA GANDHI

A FEW HEARTFELT THANK YOUS

To the fabulous Rowan Lawton and the team at Furniss Lawton for all their invaluable help and advice.

To Briony Gowlett, for being such an inspiring editor and having confidence in me, Louise Swannell for her super PR efforts and Caitriona Horne for marketing prowess.

To all those who help me with the continual juggling act (and often pick up the odd stray ball): To Mum, Dad and James for all their love, continual help and support; Annie, Becca, Fi, Jules, Lorna, Liana, Anna, Jess, Gemma, Amy, Ju and all my other wonderful friends (you know who you are!) for the giggles, tea and sanity-saving chats; and last but by no means least, to Chris for being a brilliant husband and dad to our girls, Arabella and Alice ('Alice, stop gurgling, Mummy is on her 'puter doing very important work!').